Published by
S.B. Nangia
A.P.H. Publishing Corporation
4435–36/7, Ansari Road, Darya Ganj,
New Delhi-110002
Phone: 011–23274050
e-mail: aphbooks@gmail.com

2026

Typeset by
Ideal Publishing Solutions
C-90, J.D. Cambridge School,
West Vinod Nagar, Delhi-110092

Printed at
DIVINE DIGITAL PRINTERS
Ansari road Daryaganj Delhi-110002

ACHIEVERS AND NON-DISCREPANT ACHIEVERS IN EDUCATION

T.V. Bindu

A.P.H. PUBLISHING CORPORATION
ANSARI ROAD, DARYA GANJ
NEW DELHI-110 002

ACKNOWLEDGEMENTS

The investigator wishes to place on record her deep sense of gratitude to Dr. Vasantha Ramkumar, Professor and Head (Retd), Department of Education, University of Kerala who guided the present research study. But for the able guidance given by her and her keen and persistent interest in the work, it would not have been possible for the investigator to complete this work. An authority on various aspects of education and educational research her profound knowledge of the area and inspiriting guidance have helped the investigator to successfully complete the study.

The investigator is also thankful to Dr.A.Sukumaran Nair former Vice-Chancellor, Mahatma Gandhi University, Kottayam for granting permission to use a number of psychometric instruments developed by him.

The investigator would also like to place on record her indebtedness to Dr.P.Viswanadhan Nair Professor and Head, Department of Education, University of Kerala who has extended all co-operation in conducting the study.

The investigator is deeply indebted to all other members of the staff who helped her in every possible way. The investigator also thanks the librarians for making available many books and periodicals for this research. The investigator also remembers with gratitude the headmasters of schools, teachers and students for the co-operation rendered in collecting the data for this study.

At the end the investigator is greatly indebted to place on record her deep sense of gratitude to all those who were behind her in executing and bringing out this thesis in the present format.

T.V. Bindu

CONTENTS

LIST OF TABLES

LIST OF FIGURES

CHAPTER 1

INTRODUCTION

Discrepant achievement has received wide research attention. Ever since its introduction, as an operational construct in educational literature, this area has emerged as a strong focus of research and diverse facets of discrepant achievement have been subjected to intense research scrutiny and critical analysis. The importance of the construct stems mainly from the fact that the incidence of one form of discrepant achievement - under achievement - is treated as an index of the functional efficiency of an educational system. Wide prevalence of under achievement in a system of education is an obvious indication that the system has failed to tap the full mental potential of a considerable proportion of its learners. The second form of discrepant achievement – over achievement - has also presented several fascinating new questions regarding mental abilities and educational performance.

The terms 'under achiever' and 'over achiever' are often misused and greatly misunderstood. The term 'under achiever' implies that the student is not working up to his potential or given ability and that the 'over achiever' is working beyond his ability. Too often teachers and parents have confused the low achiever with the under achiever and the high achiever with the over achiever.

The terms 'over' and 'under' have the connotation of being above and below something. In regard to academic achievement, these terms refer to a predictive criterion, which is usually a score on the so-called tests of intelligence. In some cases reading and achievement tests have also been added as multiple predictors. Therefore students achieving above or below their potential as indicated by one or more scores on these tests have been labeled 'over' or 'under'.

Many researchers tend to use the term 'under achievement' to describe all low academic performance and to use 'over achievement' in reference to all high grades. Actually, there are few studies on over achievement, *per se*. Most of the work has been done with high achievers, regardless of factors of prediction. Applying Shaw's rule of thumb (Miller, 1968), the underachieving group in most of the studies will be defined as the "students in the upper 25 per cent of their class with respect to intellectual ability who are falling below the class average with respect to grades". Children with lower I.Q. scores are not usually included in studies of under achievement since by definition the under achiever would have to possess a certain minimum I.Q. Therefore , most of the research will concern under achievers rather than low achievers. Because of the lack of studies on the over achiever, most of the research to be cited in contrast to the under achievers would have been done on 'high' achievers.

Research findings show that approximately half of all males who are above average in ability may be considered under achievers before they go to college. Indications of male proclivity toward under achievement in junior and senior high school can be observed as early as the third grade. Girls begin to demonstrate a lack of academic potential in the late elementary or early junior high school grades. Prior to entering college, boys outnumber girls in the under achieving group by a ratio of approximately two to one. At high school level, the sex differences in I.Q. scores are not great enough to account for this large differentiation in academic achievement. At the college level, on the other hand, the sex differentiation is not so great. In some cases girl under achievers outnumber the boys, whose motivation for high grades may have changed at this level.

As a group, under achievers have been found generally to be deficient in academic skills. They suffer from lack of attentiveness and in contrast to high achievers cannot concentrate on their studies in adverse or distracting circumstances. They do not devote enough time to their studies. Characteristically they need immediate rather than long term satisfaction. Certain compulsive and impulsive traits interfere with their performance. Gilmore (1968) has found them defensible, rigid and unable to work easily in the academic situation. Because of emotional conflicts, the intake of general information is blocked. Studies on impulse control suggest that they are more impulsive than high achievers (Merril and Murphy, Weigand, Mc Arthur and Mc David in Lavin, 1965).

Report of the Education Commission (1964-66) says that the group of underachievers consists of children who are not intellectually dull but are at least of average and may even be of superior ability. The failure of such children should be of great concern to a developing country like ours, which cannot remain indifferent to this loss of potential manpower within the high ability range. If classroom teaching is defective or does not yield the best results, we have to conclude that the country's progress will be hampered to that extent. It becomes essential, therefore, that a foolproof and more adequate system of education is developed so that wastage of all kinds - including implied wastage of intellectual potential - are reduced to a minimum. Under achievement on the part of the students is one of the main defects in the educational setup and the factors contributing to this phenomenon have to be identified, analyzed and remedial measures found out.

Over achievers are found to perform better than what is expected of them on the basis of their ability. The concept of over achievement implies that besides intelligence; there are variables, which exercise a positive influence on achievement. There is scope for certain variables, other than inherited potential, which it detected and identified, can be controlled to maximize achievement.

Several factors physical, intellectual, emotional and environmental contribute to the failure of under achievers to come up to the level of their latent abilities. Several studies conducted in India and abroad revealed that discrepant achievement in different subjects is different.

A study conducted by Deo and Gupta (1972) proposed 25 percentage over achievers 23-72 percentage normal achievers and 20-49 percentage of under achievers. Tolor (1969) made an attempt to determine the incidence of under achievement at the high school level.The incidence of under achievement was 26 per cent. Abraham (1972) made a comparative study of the incidence of under achievement and over achievement in English and has noted that 14.9 per cent are over achievers and 15.4 per cent area under achievers. Abraham (1975) in her study proposed under achievement of about 15 per cent on English. Cherian (1984) in her study of the problems faced by under achievers in secondary schools found that 13.9 percentage are under achievers and 13.3 percentage are over achievers. This study made use of Composite Test of Generalised Achievement.

Nair's (1974) study revealed that 28 per cent under achievers are there in Mathematics. Mathew (1975) reported the incidence of under achievement at secondary school level in science to be 16 per cent. Nair (1987) in his study of psychological characteristics of 'creative under achievers' in science has found that 26.6 per cent are under achievers and 14.2 per cent are overachievers in Science.

A study, at the Fels Institute, of two different I.Q. groups is important to our theoretical approach. Researchers divided 140 subjects, whose I.Q. had changed between the ages of 6 and 10 into ascenders (where the I.Q. increased) and descenders (where it decreased).

The results are interpreted as indicating that high motivation to achieve, competitive striving, and curiosity about nature may motivate the acquisition of intellectual skills and knowledge which, in turn, facilitates increases in tested I.Q. Similarly, need for achievement and successful competition should motivate attempts at improvement of intellectual abilities in a social milieu where praise, recognition, and superior status are awarded for such accomplishment. That is, achievement oriented children from homes in which intellectual activity was praised would probably be more likely to master intellectual skills than achievement oriented children from homes where such accomplishments were not rewarded. In a cultural environment where athletic ability, fighting powers, or success with the opposite sex was highly valued, one might expect the child to choose these behavioural channels to gratify his achievement and competitive needs.

NEED AND SIGNIFICANCE OF THE STUDY

The introduction of the new research construct of discrepant achievement implies the possibility of labeling any instructional group into three major categories, namely over achievers, normal achievers and under achievers. Over achievers are those whose educational performance is higher than what is expected of them on the basis of their mental ability. The two groups (Under Achievers and Over Achievers) put together are labeled as discrepant achievers - those who deviate from normal educational performance and hence perform either above or below the levels expected of them on the basis of their mental potential. The classification normally opens up a basic ethical question of the obligation of an educational system to provide appropriate instructional strategies for dealing with each of these groups and ensure that no students in an educational system is allowed to perform at a level lower than what is expected of him in terms of his measured intelligence. The acceptance of the new construct has also posed several important research questions, only a few of which have been taken up by researchers for detailed study. The two extreme groups, namely over achievers and under achievers, together classified as discrepant achievers, differ significantly from the group of normal achievers, and need to be looked upon as a single group and studied as such.

Researches on discrepant achievement conducted both in India and abroad have mostly been confined to certain limited areas within the major field. Most of these studies have been addressed to the investigation of casual factors of one form of discrepant achievement, namely, under achievement, in defined curriculum areas. Parallel investigations relating to over achievement are lesser in number. There has not been any attempt to probe some of the more basic question relating to discrepant achievement. For example, questions like the following have not been properly answered. What causes under achievement or over achievement in a given learning-instructional situation? Is it possible to reduce the incidence of under achievement? What kinds of educational intervention strategies would help to reduce this phenomenon? How are discrepant achievers different from normal achievers? Are factors relating to under achievement and over achievement the same or different for different curriculum areas? Will the incidence of discrepant achievement differ from subject to subject? Is the phenomenon of discrepant achievement persists over a period of time? Many such questions have not been properly answered by researchers. There has not been any attempt to evolve a comprehensive theory of discrepant achievement and consequently we have failed to evolve a model of instruction, which will reduce the incidence of under achievement, or increase the incidence of normal achievement or over achievement. Also, the related ethical psychological question of whether over achievement needs to be encouraged as an educational goal has not been adequately investigated since the phenomenon of over achievement has not been studied properly or has not been brought under a comprehensive theory of discrepant achievement.

Existing studies help us to understand certain basic dimensions related to under achievement which include psychological dimensions like motivation, adjustment and attitudes, social and other environmental dimensions, persona -demographic variables like age, gender of subjects, family size, order of birth etc. The factors, which cause under achievement, can be concerned to fall outside the realm of cognitive domain since the concept of under achievement itself takes into account a major portion of the cognitive potential of the individuals. But a large number of recent studies in this area have indicated that non -cognitive variables including personal and familial factors also contribute the phenomenon of discrepant achievement. We have number of studies, which indicate factors associated with different forms of under achievement. They can be classified broadly under the following major groups:

(i) ***Intelligence factors:*** low intelligence, absence of basic language skills, poor reasoning ability.

(ii) ***Personality factors***: adjustment, achievement motivation, masculinity-femininity, anxiety.

(iii) ***Socio-personal factors***: Socio-economic status, rural-urban residence, social backwardness, cultural milieu, family relations.

The relation between under achievement and intelligence has been demonstrated by studies like those of Thorndike (1963), Burt (1966), Anadavally (1972), Mohan and Nehru (1972), Vernon (1972) Nair (1974), Iyer (1977), Abraham (1978), Cherian (1984) Klein (1984), Mehrotra (1986), Ford (1992), Mathew (1993),Ford (1997).

The relation between personality factors and under achievement is indicated by studies like those of Joshi and Sharma (1968), Dhaliwal (1971), Saxena (1972), Sharma (1972), Sathi (1973), Nair (1974), Mathew (1975), Joseph (1977), Singh and Kumar (1977),

Abraham (1978), Najma and Satyanarayana (1978) Blusiewiea (1983), Haq (1988), Hawkins (1992), Shoba (1993), Klinger and Nelson (1996).

The role of socio-familial factors on under achievement have been investigated by studies like those of Srivastava (1967), Abraham (1975), Mathew (1975), Joseph (1977), Iyer (1977), Nair (1981), Cherian (1984), Nair (1987), Nair (1987) Uchat (1987), Wilkie (1992), Skinner (1994), Baum (1995), Chen *et al* (1995), Grayson (1996), Paul (1996), Nord (1998). Among the family environment variables, only peripheral variables like income level, occupational level etc been covered. Most of these studies have not taken into consideration have the effect of deeper variables like cultural level of the family, acceptance of education by the family, home learning facilities available etc.

Parallel studies have been conducted to identify similar dimensions associated with over achievement.

The studies quoted above are isolated studies, which refer to certain aspects of cognitive, affective and social-familial variables related to under achievement. No attempt has been made to study the effect of certain important psycho-familial variables associated with discrepant achievement in various school subjects. Apart from delineating the role of certain conventional generalized achievement-facilitating and achievement-debilitating factors in causing under achievement or over achievement, there has not been a concerted and comprehensive effort to answer many of the other major questions which would lead to a better understanding of the nature of discrepant achievement.

It is obvious from the preceding discussions that more systematic investigations are needed to obtain a wide comprehensive understanding of the phenomenon in respect of its relative incidence in different groups and identifying its causal factors. All major variables associated with the phenomenon intellectual variables, personality variables, social-familial and other environmental variables have not been properly studied. Yet another subject gap in existing research relates to the identification of subjects who are discrepant achievers in a number of important curriculum areas. If under achievement of a subject in any one curriculum area is an indication of wasted educational effort, than under achievement in a number of curriculum areas should be looked upon as much more serious drawback of the educational set up. Researches, which help to identify some of the major psycho-familial variables of discrepant achievement in various school subjects, would be invaluable in extending the frontiers of knowledge relating to the phenomenon of discrepant achievement. The present research is, therefore, intended to study the association of certain important psychological and familial variables with discrepant achievement with respect to six curriculum areas - Mother Tongue (Malayalam), English, Hindi, Social Studies, Science and Mathematics. Hence, the present study is intended to obtain a very comprehensive picture of some major psychological and familial dimensions associated with discrepant achievement in various secondary school subjects using data obtained from a single group of subjects, obtained using common testing instruments.

STATEMENT OF THE PROBLEM

The problem taken up for study has been worded as:

A Comparative Study of Discrepant Achievers and Non Discrepant Achievers in Secondary School Subjects in Relation to Certain Psychological and Familial Variables.

DEFINITION OF TERMS

The important terms used in the study are defined below:

Discrepant Achievers and Non Discrepant Achievers

The term 'under achievers' stands for those whose educational performances is lower than what is expected of them on the basis of their mental ability. Similarly 'over achievers' are those whose educational performance is higher than what is expected of them on the basis of their mental ability. The two groups put together are labeled as 'discrepant achievers' – those who deviate from normal educational performance and hence perform either above or below the levels expected of them on the basis of their mental potential. Those who are not belonging to any of these two categories are labeled as 'non discrepant achievers.'

Secondary School

Any school recognized by the Government of Kerala for giving instructions to students at the terminal stage of school education (Standard VIII, IX and X).

Psychological Variables

Psychological variables, as used in the study, stand for a representative set of affective variables, accepted as belonging to the domain of personality in modern psychological dimensions. Seven personality variables have been selected to stand for the term psychological variables.

Familial variables

A group of variables, which describe various aspects of an individual's family environment. The familial variables as used in the study include Family Cultural Level, Home Environment, Family Acceptance of Education and Home Learning Facility.

Variables of the Study

The study has been designed with discrepant – non discrepant continuum as the "dependent variable". Independent variables of the study can be classified into two groups namely, Psychological and Familial variables as detailed below:

Psychological variables

Personal Adjustment

Social Adjustment

General Anxiety

Examination Anxiety

Introversion – extraversion

Masculinity – femininity

Achievement Motivation

Familial Variables

Family Education Level

Family Cultural Level

Family Environment

Family Acceptance

Home Learning Facility.

HYPOTHESES

The study has been designed round the following hypotheses.

1. Each of the independent variables selected for study will discriminate significantly between Discrepant Achievers (Under Achievers) and Non Discrepant Achievers in Six school subjects (Malayalam, English, Hindi, Social Studies, Science, and Mathematics).

2. Each of the independent variables selected for study will discriminate significantly between Discrepant Achievers (Over Achievers) and Non Discrepant Achievers in Six school subjects (Malayalam, English, Hindi, Social Studies, Science, and Mathematics).

Objectives of the Study

The hypotheses set for the study helped the investigator to define the specific objectives of the study. The following are the objectives of the study :

(i) To compare each of the Psychological and Familial variables of Discrepant Achievers (Under Achievers) and Non Discrepant Achievers (NDA) in Six school subjects.

The comparison to be made for the following contrasted groups:

DA (UA)	–	NDA (Malayalam)
DA (UA)	–	NDA (English)
DA (UA)	–	NDA (Hindi)
DA (UA)	–	NDA (Social Studies)
DA (UA)	–	NDA (Science)
DA (UA)	–	NDA (Mathematics)

(ii) To compare each of the Psychological and Familial variables of Discrepant Achievers (Over Achievers) and Non Discrepant Achievers (NDA) in Six school subjects.

The comparisons to be made for the following contrasted groups:

DA (OA)	-	NDA (Malayalam)
DA (OA)	-	NDA (English)
DA (OA)	-	NDA (Hindi)
DA (OA)	-	NDA (Social Studies)
DA (OA)	-	NDA (Science)
DA (OA)	-	NDA (Mathematics)

Methodology

(a) Sample

The data for the study has been derived from a representative sample of size 879 obtained from Standard IX pupils attending schools of Thiruvananthapuram, Pathanamthitta and Kottayam Districts of the State of Kerala. The sample was obtained using stratified random sampling procedure with due representation given to factors like school efficiency, rural – urban residence of subjects, sex of subjects, institutional type etc. The basal sample was divided into Under Achievers, Over Achievers and Non Discrepant Achievers separately in six school subjects, namely, Malayalam, English, Hindi, Social Studies, Science and Mathematics using Regression equation.

(b) Tools

The data for the study has been obtained using a group of standardized psychometric instruments like tests of verbal and non-verbal intelligence, personality measures like tests of socio – personal adjustments, anxiety, motivation, tests of socio-economic status, family environment measures, achievement test in various school subjects. All the tools used are popular instruments of proved validity and reliability.

(c) Statistical techniques used

The following statistical techniques are used for analysis:

(i) Farquhar's Regression Technique for identifying Discrepant Achievers in various school subjects; and

(ii) Two – tailed tests of significance for difference between means of large independent samples for comparison of groups.

Scope and Limitations of the Study

The descriptions of the study attempted above are mostly adequate to convey the scope and limitations of the study. But, since they have been presented in combination with other routine descriptions, the investigator decided to make a more detailed analysis of the scope and limitations. The important aspects that need special mention in this context are the following:

(1) The study, as stated in earlier contexts, has been designed with 'discrepant – non discrepant continuum' as the dependent variable and a set of Psychological and Familial variables as independent variables. The selection of the variables under each category has been done giving due consideration to the fact that they should have a reasonable chance of being related to

under achievement, over achievement and normal achievement. The decision was taken on the basis of available research findings and theoretical indications. The investigator presumes that the coverage of variables is broad enough to obtain a reasonably dependable and generalisable perspective of the problem under investigation – identification of certain dominant variables associated with Discrepant Achievers and Non Discrepant Achievers in various school subjects.

(2) A total of twelve Psychological and Familial variables (seven Psychological and five Familial variables) have been selected for the present study. It cannot be claimed that they are exhaustive and that they represent all the dimensions of Psychological variables and Familial variables. However, it needs to be stated that many of the construct of personality have been confined to certain major areas of personality – social and personal dimensions, motivational dimensions, anxiety dimensions, etc.

(3) The sample of the study is a representative group of secondary school pupils – pupils of Standard IX – drawn from select schools of Thiruvananthapuram, Pathanamthitta and Kottayam Districts of Kerala State. The confining of the study to these districts has not in any way decreased the generalizability of the study because these districts contain schools of almost all degrees of efficiency and contain all shades of pupils and hence can provide a representative sample of secondary school children of the State of Kerala. The confining of the study to pupils of Standard IX was governed by the consideration that Standard IX will best represent Standards VIII, IX and X, which forms the secondary stage in the school systems of Kerala. Standard X is not normally available for group testing in view of the busy schedule of the schools for preparing their pupils for the State Public Examination.

(4) The regression technique has been used to classify the sample into Under Achievers, Over Achievers and Non Discrepant Achievers in various school subjects with two intelligence measures, namely, a verbal and a non – verbal tests of intelligence and a standardized test battery of achievement test containing six school subjects (namely, English, Malayalam, Hindi, Social Studies, Science and Mathematics developed specially for pupils of standard IX of Kerala) used for classification. The results are valid and generalizable within the limits set by the techniques adopted for measurement and classification. It may be noted that all the tests used are standardized instruments and the method of classification is also the most satisfactory techniques in existence.

(5) The decision regarding the statistical techniques was taken keeping a number of crucial factors in view. The method used for identifying the variables which can discriminate between Discrepant Achievers (Under Achievers and Over Achievers) and Non Discrepant Achievers in various school subjects was adopted with strict regard to the nature of data in view. A sharper test of significance, viz, Analysis of Variance was given up since it requires that the scores analysed should satisfy certain basic criteria. The Critical Ratio tests, on the other hand, are more flexible in that the test imposes fewer conditions on the distribution of the variables. The factors related to Discrepant Achievement and Non Discrepant Achievement have been identified with the help of tests of significance for difference between means.

Though maximum effort has been taken to make the study as generalisable as possible, a few minor limitations have crept into the study. Most of these limitations are inherent in almost all forms of behavioural and social science research of the present kind. While attempts have been made to minimize the errors accruing from such experimental sources, it cannot be claimed that such errors have been completely eliminated. However, these limitations have been borne in mind in interpreting the findings.

While owning the limitations, the investigator claims that the findings of the present study will be of use to teachers, parents and other concerned educational workers in understanding the causes of discrepant achievement from subject to subject, the solutions to reduce the phenomenon of under achievement etc. It is hoped that the obtained knowledge will be of help in understanding the interaction between important personality and familial variables and discrepant and non discrepant achievers in various school subjects of secondary school pupils. This may help to plan suitable educational environment when dealing with the causes of discrepant achievement and its remediation.

Organization of the Report

The report has been presented in six chapters.

The introductory chapter (Chapter I) presents a rationale for selecting the present problem, its significance, special functions of the study, definition of the problem and key terms used, statement of the hypotheses and objectives of the study, and a brief discussion of the scope and limitations of the study.

The second chapter (Chapter II) presents a theoretical overview of discrepant achievement, which included over achievers and under achievers

The next chapter (Chapter III) presents a detailed review of select literature from the areas of academic achievement, under achievement, over achievement, psychological and familial variables related to discrepant achievement

Chapter IV of the report describes the methodology of the study details relating to measuring tools, sample, collection of data and statistical techniques employed.

The next chapter (Chapter V) presents details regarding analysis of data taken up in the order objectives of the study. The analysis has been followed by the interpretation of the major findings.

The last chapter (Chapter VI) presents a short resume of the study, major conclusions educational implications of findings and suggestions for further research.

CHAPTER 2

DISCREPANT ACHIEVEMENT : A THEORETICAL OVERVIEW

In this chapter an attempt has been made to present a theoretical overview of various aspects associated with discrepant achievement.

THE CONCEPT OF DISCREPANT ACHIEVEMENT

The concept of discrepant achievement has been developed fully and is being used extending in the hands of researchers and classroom teachers. Discrepant achiever is one who shows discrepancy in achievement with respect to his intelligence or mental ability. This discrepancy can either be in the positive direction or in the negative direction. If it is in the positive direction it is called over achievement and if in the negative direction it is called under achievement.

UNDER ACHIEVEMENT AND OVER ACHIEVEMENT

The terms 'under achiever' and 'under achievement' need to be elucidated before any theoretical discussions of the concepts can be taken up. Estimates of the magnitude of the problem of under achievement tend to vary depending on how 'under achievement' is defined and who is included in the population under consideration.

Some of the researchers used the concept of under achievement in a narrow sense as low scholastic performance of high ability students thus excluding the average or below average from this class of students. But this phenomenon occurs at all ability levels. For any ability level, if a person achieves below what is expected of him, he is usually termed as 'under achiever'.

The term under achiever implies that the student is not working up to his potential or given ability and over achiever is working beyond his ability. While high - and low - achievement refers only to above and below average achievers, the concept of over and under achievement takes into account the academic achievement in relation to the intellectual level of the individual. Under and over achievement can be understood as the discrepancy between intelligence test scores and achievement test scores.

According to Fliegler (1957) an under achiever is a student who does not "appear to be functioning academically up to his assessed ability as determined by an individual intelligence test". In other words, an under achiever is one whose achievement is significantly less than what he is really capable of achieving by virtue of his intelligence. An under achiever is always identified in terms of some accepted external criterion which measure ability or intellectual potential or scholastic aptitude.

In a three year experiment at Dewitt Clington High School, New York City, under achievers were identified as those with IQ's of 120 and above and grades below 80 per cent (Goldberg, 1959) while in another study, under achievers were those with IQ's of 115 and above, and grades in the bottom quarters of their class (Raths, 1961).

The Education Commission (1964-66) gives a more restricted definition when they state that the group of under achievers consists of children who are not intellectually dull but are at least of average and may even be of superior ability. This definition suffers from the fact that it excludes under achieving children of low intellectual capacity. However, modern psychological literature gives the term a broad connotation by considering it as existing at all levels of intelligence, viz., high - intelligence, average - intelligence and low - intelligence. Whatever definitions accepted, the method usually employed in these studies is to test ability, test achievement and then identify those whose achievement does not measure up to their expected or potential level.

For Wellington and Wellington (1964) an under achiever has come to mean " a student who appears to possess ability to achieve considerably higher grades than his present record shows". Under achievers are students who possess good or high potential and show a discrepancy between their potential and actual achievement. An under achiever, according to Tolor (1969) is a child who has (a) at least average current intellectual functioning and (b) a placement on a standard achievement test of at least one standard error of estimate expectancy, based on his own IQ.

In their oft quoted study on talented high school students, Getzels and Jackson (1962) raised a question whether the so called over achievement may not at least in some cases be related to excellence in cognitive functions not sampled by the conventional IQ metric rather than inevitably to psycho - pathology. Their argument was based on the observation that those very high on creativity measure achieved equality as well as their lesser creative but more intelligent classmates. Torrence (1962) proposed a thorough re-examination of the concepts of over achievement and under achievement and stated that, in general, under achievement tended to have higher IQ's and lower scores on tests of creative thinking than over achievers.

Considering the methodological hazards involved in the identification of under and over achievers (students who achieve less or more than could be anticipated by their scholastic aptitude scores) and the only moderate degree of relationship between academic aptitude and school achievement it is somewhat questionable what practical utility widely used concepts have for educational practice (Thorndike 1961, 1963).

Davis (1955) in a study to characterize differences among academic under achievers of superior intelligence identified three distinct types of under achievers. They are:

(i) Withdraws from the achievement situation by denying his giftedness.

(ii) Concerned about not living up to their potential, but does not take responsibility for failure.

(iii) Prefers autonomy, enjoys learning and generally pursues his own goals.

DIFFERENT TYPES OF UNDER ACHIEVERS

There are many causes for under achievement. It is not possible to generalize very broadly about under achievement and under achievers because the difficulties are likely to differ from case to case. Otto *et al* (1973) identified six general categories in which children with achievement problems tend to be classified. The categories serve mainly to demonstrate the scope of the under achievement problem.

(i) ***Under achievers with average capacity***: On the basis of their capacity to learn, children with average intelligence are usually expected to achieve approximately at their chronological grade-placement level; those who do not, are under achievers. Any of a wide variety of learning difficulties may be responsible for failure to achieve.

(ii) ***Slow learners***: Children with IQ's between 80 and 90 are often called slow learners. A child with an average IQ (90-110) is probably an under achiever if he fails to work successfully at above grade level, a slow learner who is achieving substantially below grade level may very well be achieving to the limit of his capacity.

Some slow learners are likely to be under achievers in that they are achieving not only below grade level but also below the expected level of their limited capacity.

(iii) ***Bright under achievers***: Some children who are achieving at grade level are under achievers. Children with high IQ's have intellectual capacities that make them potentially able to achieve above the level of their chronological grade placements; when they do not, they are clearly under achievers despite the fact that they may produce fairly competent work at grade level. In practice, it is the bright under achiever who is most routinely ignored by the schools.

(iv) ***Reluctant learners***: Some children are able to attain adequate scores on achievement tests but fail to function in the classroom at a level consistent with their test scores and abilities. Such children are not likely to be located by screening attempts that are confined to comparisons of formal test scores. Reluctant learners are commonly lacking in motivation.

(v) ***Children with limited experimental backgrounds***: Many children come to school from homes that are barren of common cultural advantage and essential language experiences. A common mistake is to label such children "dull" when they fail to respond to instruction that is alien to most of their previous experiences. Unless these children get the special help they need early in their school experience, most of them are likely to emerge as under achievers in the early grades.

(vi) ***Children with limited language development***: Nevertheless, language development *per se* has been receiving considerable attention from many workers and there is no questioning that lack of adequate language development can be seriously delimiting factor in children's achievement.

UNDER ACHIEVEMENT DISTINGUISHED FROM OVER ACHIEVEMENT

The term over and under achievement are sometimes confused with high - and low - achievement. The concept of high - and low - achievement are defined in terms of performance with respect to an absolute standard of performance while over and under achievement involve the discrepancy between predicted and actual performance. According to Farewell and Peters (1969) under achievement refers to that level of accomplishment, which does not measure up to the potential capability of the individual. Over achievement would stand for a level of achievement, which is considerably higher than the individuals' potential for achievement as computed by conventional scholastic aptitude tests. Under achievement points out that a potential indicated by ability is not being realized, and that the factors that militate against its realization have to be exposed. Over achievers are pupils whose school attainment is in excess of expectations formed on the basis of their ability. In this case, obviously we would not say that such pupils ought to be performing in accordance with their ability, since an over riding concern of both teachers and psychologists in the maximization of performance. But the concept of over achievement suggests that besides intelligence, there are variables, which exercise a positive influence on achievement. This leads to the question of identifying the variables, and testing whether they are absent in under achievers and whether under achievers possess characteristics, which are absent in over achievers.

Taylor (1964) in his review of research on relationship between certain personality traits and discrepant achievement suggested that there were seven 'traits', which are related to over and under achievers. They are:

(i) the over achiever has less anxiety than the under achiever and great self-control, which would enable him to direct his anxiety to constructive end.

(ii) the over achiever has positive feelings of self-worth whereas the under achiever is poorly adjusted and lacks self-confidence.

(iii) conformity to authority is more characteristic of the over achiever than the under achiever.

(iv) the over achiever is more concerned with social acceptance than the under achiever and tends to have positive relation with peers.

(v) the over achiever tends to have less conflict over issues concerning dependence and independence than the under achiever.

(vi) the over achiever is academically rather than socially oriented in his activities, and

(vii) the over achiever is more realistic in his choice of goals than the under achiever.

Though the concept of over achievement and under achievement have been very popular at the hands of educators, many criticisms about the theoretical assumptions are seen in the work of a number of researchers. Many are of opinion that these phenomena are due basically to 'the imperfectness of our predictions' (Thorndike, 1963). Some writers consider that these phenomena are to be explained in terms of 'artifacts of measurement' (Coleman and Curelon,1954). Some others submitted that the deviant achievement patterns are a function more of school policy than of individual pupil's characteristics (Kowit and Armstrong, 1961).

Torrance (1962) has come forward with the suggestion that the concept of over achievement and under achievement have to be re-examined thoroughly. According to him, under achievers tended to have higher IQ's and lower scores on tests of creative thinking than over achievers. Vernon (1972) points out that low-intelligence and generally unfavorable environment are far more important causes of under achievement, than is malnutrition, which some educators consider as a major cause of low-achievement.

Lee and Siegal (1960) observed that the term 'over achiever' may be questioned because of the implication that the student does more than what he is capable of doing. The term 'over achievement' sounds absurd, for it seems to mean performance better than what the 'person is able to do.' The same reasoning can be applied to under achievement, but it is rarely done, because it is easier to imagine one getting a lower score than he should on an aptitude test.

Lowther (1962) even goes to the extent of saying that the term over achievement is an irrational concept and, therefore, it should be discarded. He points out three major misconceptions. They are :

(1) motivation is not seen as a variety of forces, which can take the form of multi-factor causality but rather is conceived as a single causal agent.

(2) Operational definitions of over and under achievement are not sufficiently scrutinized.

(3) the term over and under achievement are imparted with a mystical discreteness instead of being viewed as extremes in a continuum.

Gowan (1964) has found that in spite of such realizations and many of the counter arguments about these concepts, many school workers are seriously concerned about the practicability of 'curing' over achievement and under achievement, though the results in the main have not been very encouraging.

IDENTIFICATION OF UNDER ACHIEVERS

Under achievement is a crucial problem that needs urgent solution so as to enable a society to derive optimum benefits from the system of education. Though it is necessary to identify under achievement at different stages during the course of a student's educational career, there is a strong argument that it is very unfair to label a youngster as 'under achiever' because once he is labeled, the individual is labeled for life, and very often the label is erroneous in many respects. Wellington and Wellington (1961) ascertain that their experience with under achievers seems to show that these students are not happy to be labeled as under achievers. However, the label appears to be essential so that it may enable us to sort out under achievers and may help us to deal with their special problems. According to Wellingtons the guess that a child is an under achiever is not enough; because guesses even by professionals have been proved to be wrong by researchers.

Various methods such as keen observation, interrogation and the use of most sophisticated statistical techniques employing psychological tests and materials are used for identifying under achievers. But the problem of identification of under achievers is not an easy task or a simple one. According to Deo (1968) the question of identifying under achievers is not so easy to answer, though the concept of under achievement sounds simple enough that 'achievement which is below the level expected on the basis of intelligence'. The slow progress of research on under achievement compared to the pace of research on normal achievement is due to this difficulty. The following two tasks are involved in the identification of under achievement:

(1) The determination of what is expected of each individual by appropriate means,

(2) The determination of the point, which marks under achievement, that is to say, how much lower than the expected achievement should the upper limit of under achievement be.

According to Naylor (1972) in identifying under achievers one has to rely heavily on the empirical relationship between IQ and attainment. Annesley *et al* (1970) has confirmed the view of Farquhar and Payne (1964) that there is a vast difference in the absolute number of achievers labeled as under achievers or over achievers depending on which definition is employed. It may be noted that the view expressed by different researches are not comparable. The varied definitions and techniques employed, together with the different sampling techniques adopted and the achievement areas studied make the comparison difficult.

METHODS OF CLASSIFYING UNDER ACHIEVERS

Different educational researchers have made use of different methods for classifying subjects into normal, over and underachievers (ie, discrepant achievers). Many statistical techniques are now widely employed for identifying the different achievement levels. Farquhar and Payne (1964) have found that all the statistical techniques now in use could be classified as follows:

(i) The central tendency split method

(ii) The method of arbitrary partition

(iii) The ranking method for ability and achievement

(iv) The regression method of selection.

In the Central Tendency Split method, achievement is dichotomized. Those high in ability and low in achievement are considered as "under achievers" and those low in ability and high in achievement are over achievers. In the second method the middle group is eliminated. In the third method achievement and ability scores are ranked separately. Over and under achievement are established as a result of discrepancy between the two ranks. The fourth method, Regression Model Selection, involves predicting achievement scores from scores on ability tests. A few important methods developed for classifying a group into over, normal and under achievers is discussed below:

I. Achievement within one standard deviation of intelligence

An assumption made in this method is that a child will be an adequate achiever if his achievement and intelligence T - scores are within one standard deviation of each other. On the other hand, if the achievement T - score of a subject is more than one standard deviation above the mean while the intelligence T - score is only within one standard deviation of the mean that subject is an over achiever. A subject is an under achiever if his achievement T - score is below one standard deviation of the mean when his intelligence T - score is within one standard deviation of the mean. When the intelligence T - score of a subject is two standard deviations above the mean he is an over achiever if his achievement T - score is more than two standard deviations above the mean and an under achiever if his achievement T - score is less than one standard deviation above the mean and so on.

II. Difference between intelligence and achievement scores relative to standard error of measurement

In this method a subject's intelligence T-score is subtracted from his achievement T-score. If this difference, whether positive or negative falls within one standard error of measurement of the intelligence test, the subject is an 'adequate achiever'. A positive difference greater than one standard error of measurement, the subject will be considered an 'over achiever'. A negative difference greater than one standard error of measurement, the subject will be considered to be an 'under achiever'.

III. Comparison of quartile ranks in achievement and intelligence

In this method an individual's quartile rank in intelligence and achievement are separately worked out and compared. Thus, if a subject has the same quartile rank in both intelligence and achievement tests, he is a 'normal achiever'. If the quartile rank in achievement is above the quartile rank in intelligence, he is an over achiever. If the quartile rank is less than the quartile rank in intelligence, he is an under achiever.

IV. Difference between actual and predicted achievement using regression equations

This is the most sophisticated technique developed for identifying under achievement and over achievement. This method was based on the work of Thorndike (1963). Regression equations were developed for criterion groups (boys' and girls') to obtain predictions of achievement from ability. Regression lines are drawn on the basis of the relation between intelligence and achievement and is used for prediction of achievement. If a student's actual achievement scores exceeded his predicted score by more than one standard error of estimate he would be designated an 'over achiever', if it fell short of the prediction by one standard error of estimate of the predicted score, he was considered as an ' under achiever', if it fell within one standard error of estimate of the predicted score, he was considered an ' adequate achiever' or 'normal achiever'

Different researchers, who have studied under achievement viz., Abraham (1973), Nair (1974), Iyer (1977), Cherian (1984), Nair (1987), Shoba (1993) and Mini Mathew (1993) have all used the regression method in their studies to sort out discrepant achievers.

Deo and Gupta (1972) have conducted a study to compare the criteria for identifying over achiever. This study suggests a disagreement between different methods with respect to identification. The regression method, T - score ratio and regression put the least number of cases as over achievers and the maximum number of 17 has been categorized by percentile method for both verbal and non-verbal basis. This indicates that the percentile method is likely to identify more students as over achievers. Variation in the average achievers ranges from 23 per cent to 72 percent. The regression method puts the maximum number of cases in this category while the least number comes from the teacher's identification. It also appears that the teachers directly identify students as over, average and under achievers, they tend to classify majority of the students in the under achiever's category which is not corroborated by the figures obtained in the other methods.

Parsley *et al* (1964) administered the California Test of Mental Maturity (CTMM), and the California Achievement Test (CAT) Battery to 3551 pupils in grades four through eight. Pupils were classified according to sex and IQ. Five IQ groups were formed on the basis of the CTMM (75 - 94, 95 - 104, 105 - 114, 115 - 124 and 125 up). The investigators selected Reading Comprehension and Reading Vocabulary grade placement scores from the CAT. The mean of these grade placement scores within each IQ sub-groups was then computed and the standard error was subtracted from each mean. All subjects with achievement scores falling ± 0. 6 grade placement points were classified 'achievers', those falling above the mean by +0.6 grade placement points were classified as 'over achievers' and those falling below – 0.6 grade placement points were classified as 'under achievers'.

Bachtold (1969) identified under achievers using the quartile technique in which the achievement and intelligence are compared using quartiles. Abraham (1969) has used the quartile technique for her study of environmental variables related to under achievement in English. Here achievement and intelligence of any individual are compared using quartiles. According to this technique, a pupil who falls into the fourth quartile in his intelligence score and into the third or second or fist quartile in his achievement score is taken to be an 'under achiever'. At the same time those student who fall into the same quartile both with reference to intelligence and achievement would be classified as 'normal achiever',

INCIDENCE OF UNDER ACHIEVEMENT

The extent of under achievement among school children has not yet been identified. The incidence of under achievement is not seen to be alike in all cases. There is variation from one sample to another, depending upon several factors associated with the sample studied. It is quite possible that the tools employed and the techniques adopted for classification will also decide the incidence of under achievement for various groups. It is likely to depend also on the efficiency of the school system. It is also dependent to a very large extent on the effectiveness of the teacher. The factors, which cause under achievement in one subject, need not necessarily cause under achievement in another subject. Accurate data concerning the incidence of under achievement are not generally available. There have been many studies of under achievement, where different definitions are used, but results of these studies are often strikingly similar.

According to Gowan (1964) a 15 per cent under achievement among gifted students is a 'normal experience'. A follow up study of 4900 'bright high school students' in New York city, brought to light the fact that half-way through school 54 per cent of the boys and 33 per cent of the girls scored low averages at school, that it was doubtful if they would get admission to a college.

Bricklin and Bricklin (1966) suggest that 15 per cent to 40 per cent of all school children fall under the category of under achievers.

Under achievers occurring at various levels of intelligence have been studied. In a study, Sharma (1972) has reported that the incidence of under achievement among high and average ability students has been found to be 50 per cent and 10 per cent respectively.

Tolor (1969) has conducted a study to determine the incidence of underachievement at the high school level. Using regression equations, the students were classified into over, normal and under achievers. The incidence of under achievement was found to be around 26 per cent with the National Educational Development Test Scores as achievement criterion.

Research studies by Nair (1974) noticed that nearly 28 percent of the high intelligence group underachieve. Mathew (1975) in his study found that about 14 per cent of the secondary school students underachieve in science. Iyer (1977) found 14 per cent secondary school students underachieve in mathematics. Abraham (1973) made a study of the factors relating to underachievement in English. She found 15 per cent were under achievers in English. In a study by Cherian (1984) it was noticed that out of 650 secondary school students 90 are under achievers (14 per cent). In another study Nair (1987) found 26.6 per cent under achievers and 14.2 over achievers in secondary school science.

Theory of under achievement based on the interaction of achievement facilitating and achievement debilitating variables

Thus there is no infirmity in the studies regarding the incidence of under achievement. The earlier and techniques used for measuring under achievement also vary considerably. The situation is as Havighurst et *al* (1955) suggest that at least half of our best human material is not developed to anywhere near capacity'. This lack of development capacity, termed 'under achievement' is alarming and poses a special situation to all interested in education.

Mathew (1975) has suggested a theory of under achievement based on achievement facilitating variables. According to him the personality variables, which in isolation help in better achievement could act in combination in such a way, that it will lead to over achievement. Higher social and personal adjustment in combination with factors like good family background, high teacher effectiveness, etc. will help a subject to show social performance well in excess of what is expected on the basis of his cognitive potential. This is what is designed as over achievement. The opposite situation will explain the incidence of under achievement. The presence of personality variables which are negatively related to achievement in combination with other factors like low teacher effectiveness, poor family background, etc. in a subject could lead to achievement well below the level expected on the basis of his cognitive potential. The resulting performance is termed under achievement. When the effects of 'achievement facilitating' and 'achievement debilitating' variables present in an individual balance each other, the subject is able to perform at the same level as would be expected on the basis of measured cognitive performance. The arguments considered above can be summarized as below :

(a) ***Over achievement***: The cumulative effect of all the achievement facilitating variables are well in excess of the cumulative effect of the achievement debilitating variables. The subject shows performance in excess of his measured intellectual potential.

(b) ***Normal achievement***: The cumulative effects of the achievement facilitating variables and the achievement debilitating variables balance each other. The subject shows performance at par with his measured intellectual potential.

(c) ***Under achievement***: The cumulative effect of the achievement debilitating variables is well in excess of the cumulative effect of the achievement facilitating variables. The subject shows performance well below his measured intellectual potential.

FACTORS AFFECTING UNDER ACHIEVEMENT

Over achievement and under achievement arises from many factors, most of them are either independent or interrelated depending on the variables used in the study. Theoretically any one or any combination of two or more factors can cause under achievement.

All these factors causing under achievement can be classified into different categories like psychological, intellectual, instructional, emotional and affective factors, individual, environmental and so on. The extent of under achievement varies in accordance with these factors. There are several studies, which purport to study broad patterns or combination of factors that lead to underachievement.

According to Pearlman (1960) college achievement of high ability students is related to:

(i) maturity and seriousness of interests

(ii) awareness and concern for others

(iii) a sense of responsibility

(iv) dominance, persuasiveness and self-confidence

(v) motivation to achieve

According to Cruickshank and Johnson (1974) characteristics of individual with high mental ability are

(i) maturity

(ii) friendly and outgoing

(iii) happy and secure

(iv) anxious and depressed

Research investigations have been shown that the negative attitude of the under achieving student is closely related to family attitudes and values.

Gough (1955) suggests that the chronic under achiever has an asocial personality and rejects school as part of a total pattern of rejecting the values of society. Under achievers showed a more negative attitude to school, work and imagination than over achievers.

The result of the study by Shaw (1966) indicated that the under achievers appeared different from the normal and over achievers in exhibiting a greater negative self-concept and a generally more negative outlook on life.

Goldberg (1959) found that under achievers has low aspiration level.

Marrow and Wilson (1961) in a study point out that under achievers were found to be too socially oriented and too active.

Robert (1962) noticed that over and under achievers differ significantly with regard to their school adjustment. Taylor (1964) has reported that under achievers are seen to identify themselves with a peer group from which they always get support.

According to Dhaliwal (1971) the important characteristics of over and under achievers are:

(i) over achievers have superior study habits

(ii) reserved ness

(iii) high verbal ability

(iv) low emotional and school adjustment

(v) poor social adjustment

(vi) high security feeling

According to Gowan (1957) under achievers are characterised by :

(i) inferior study habits

(ii) outgoing tendencies

(iii) low verbal ability

(iv) emotional instability

(v) assertiveness

(vi) happy go like temperament

(vii) poor adjustment home, emotional and school areas

(viii) good social adjustment

(ix) insecurity feelings.

In a study by Fink (1962) the under achieving girls appear to be poorly controlled and impulsive. The under achieving boys appear to be the "most inadequate and immature". They also feel socially left out. They do not hold to the ideals, values and goals of the dominant cultural groups.

In a study by Mitchell (1959) the "self-acceptant" under achievers fulfill their ego-needs in areas other than academic are not willing to exert much effort in order to achieve.

The self-acceptant overachievers are well-adjusted, good students who aspire for higher grades and who see themselves as mature, worthy, well-linked persons.

The self - rejectant under achievers are the least motivated of all and cannot keep their mind on their work.

Personality characteristics common to under achievers of both sexes are :

(i) they suffer from a weak ego

(ii) they have greater amount of hostility towards themselves and others than over achievers

(iii) they would rationalize their poor study habits and reading disabilities

(iv) they have feelings of inadequacy insecurity and fear of failure.

(v) they suffer from lack of attentiveness

(vi) they need immediate satisfaction

Gowan (1964) has concluded from the studies on under achievement that the following factors are related to under achievement:

(i) lack of clearness and definiteness of academic and occupational choice.

(ii) weak ego controls

(iii) withdrawal and self-sufficiency

(iv) poor uses of time and money

(v) neurotic tendencies

(vi) authoritarianism in the parental home or the individual himself

(vii) dominant, autocratic or laissez-faire parents

(viii) no goals or impossible demands by parents

(ix) lack of maturity and irresponsibility

(x) disinterest in other people

(xi) lack of dominance, persuasiveness and self-confidence

(xii) apathetic and withdrawing view of life.

Barett (1957) felt that under achievement results from a feeling of insecurity and inadequacy accompanied by hostility.

According to Wellington and Wellington (1964) the following factors seem to exist in the case of under achievers:

(i) low study motivation

(ii) low sense of responsibility

(iii) low dominance

(iv) low self – confidence

(v) low capacity to work under pressure

(vi) low concern for others

(vii) not able to set goals for themselves about their study and their educational future.

The specific causes for under achievement in mathematics, according to Shaw (1966) are the following :

(i) causes pertaining to teachers

(ii) causes pertaining to pupils

(iii) causes pertaining to curriculum, and

(iv) causes pertaining to school administration.

Mehta (1975) conducted a study on the causes of low achievement in study among intellectually normal school children.

From the analysis and interpretation of the data through case study of 30 selected pupils the investigator could find out the following factors, which adversely affected the pupils' achievement. They are:

(i) the home environment

(ii) lack of encouragement and proper educational guidance

(iii) poor economic condition of parents

(iv) lack of interest of parents

(v) distance of home from school, and

(vi) inadequate curriculum .

Desana (1966) reveals that under achievers' chief problem areas are:

(i) adjustment to college work

(ii) social and recreational activities

(iii) social and psychological relations

(iv) future vocational planning

(v) personal and psychological relations

The study also noticed that under achievers show greater willingness to discuss their problems if opportunities were provided.

Although many studies have found little or no difference in the personality traits of under and over achievers, other studies have isolated certain characteristics, which may differentiate them. According to Wellington (1964) under achievers show a tendency to procrastinate, seem to have less self-confidence, more negativity toward school, less interest in reading, and withdrawal from competition. They are said to lack good use of time and money, show psychotic or neurotic tendencies set either no goals or impossible ones, feel disinterested in others and lack an enthusiastic socialized activity-oriented view of life.

Major factors contributing to under achievement obtained by summarizing the available research findings are given below:

(1) poor home environment

(2) indifferent family

(3) parental conflict

(4) sterility in affection

(5) lack of attention

(6) poor physique

(7) low self-concept

(8) lack of motivation

(9) poor emotional adjustment

(10) faulty learning and bad study habits

(11) more interest in extra-curricular and non-academic activities.

Ordinarily we would have to say either that the highly creative group was "over achieving" and working too hard or that the high - IQ group was "under achieving" and out to work harder. Teachers, however, related the highly creative as less ambitious and less hard working. Under achieving gifted child has not made use of his abilities in socially acceptable channels.

EDUCATIONAL IMPLICATIONS

Many studies have been conducted to given an answer to the question "how underachievement could be minimized"? Farewell and Peters (1966) specifically state the need of guidance and counseling with under achievers. Several causes such as environmental, instructional and personal were examined to see which of these cause under achievement. Kaul (1968) concluded that if the parents co-operate with teachers in helping the students make proper use of study hours through guided assignments at home and through correlative remedial teaching measures at school in weak areas, under achievement could be reduced to some extent.

Abraham (1973) in her study concluded that scholastic under achievement appears to be associated with a complex of factors and has to be dealt with on an individual basis.

Several studies like those of Broed *et al* (1960), Caplan (1957), Cohen (1963) have explored the effectiveness of multiple counseling in working with secondary school students. But there are other studies, which do not clearly indicate that counseling has a positive effect on under achievers.

According to Gowan (1964) gifted under achiever is "a kind of intellectual delinquent who withdraws from goals, activities and active social participation generally.

Studies on discrepant achievement help in identifying groups like under achieving gifted children during the early years in school. The following are some of the implications:

(i) assigning tutors to support and to motivate the children through success in academic achievement. This can be done more readily on a one to one basis than in a classroom situation.

(ii) counselling with the parents concerning the problems of the child and attempting to develop better home relations.

(iii) rewarding the child by praise and recognition in school for efforts and achievement in academic work.

(iv) organizing small special classes for the under achieving gifted children with special teachers, preferably male if the predominance of such children are mostly boys.

When the child is gifted but under achieving special attention to his social and emotional problems or possible areas of weakness is called for. Intensive counseling and parent education or even remedial instruction may be more important for this child than his placement.

STUDIES ON UNDER ACHIEVEMENT IN KERALA

The study of under achievement as an organized school of research is in evidence in the Department of Education, University of Kerala. The early studies go back to about 25 years when A.S. Nair and his associates (1974), Abraham (1974), Mathew (1975), Joseph (1977), Iyer (1977), Cherian (1984), Nair (1987), Shoba (1993), Mini Mathew (1993) and quite a few others - gave a new direction to research in this area. Studies are mostly directed to the identification of causal factors of under achievement in certain school subjects like Science, Mathematics etc. A good number of researches - both at the postgraduate and doctoral level - have been conducted under the guidance and supervision of A.S. Nair. The important studies of this team have been reviewed in Chapter III of the present report.

CHAPTER 3

REVIEW OF RELATED LITERATURE

This session deals with a brief review of certain relevant research studies, which have direct or indirect bearing on the phenomenon of discrepant achievement. The major focus of the present study is to study the group differences in the incidence of discrepant achievement in terms of certain important Psychological and Familial variables. The review will, therefore, be confined to only those studies, which explore the association between Discrepant Achievement and certain Psychological and Familial variables used for the present study. The important studies of this kind, are presented below :

PSYCHOLOGICAL AND FAMILIAL VARIABLES IN RELATION TO DISCREPANT AND NON DISCREPANT ACHIEVEMENT

A review of studies relating to this part helps the investigator to study the relationship between under and over achievement and a number of psychological and familial variables. These studies cover variables like parental education, parental occupation, socio-economic status, home environment, parent-child relationship, anxiety, motivation etc.

Roberts (1962) noticed that over and underachievers differ significantly with regard to their school adjustment.

In their of quoted study on talented high school students Getzels and Jackson (1962) questioned whether the "so called over achievement may not at least in some cases be related to excellence in cognitive functions not sampled by the conventional IQ metric rather than inevitably to psycho-pathology". They observed that those very high on creativity measure achieved equality as well as their lesser creative but more intelligent classmates.

According to Torrance (1962) under achievers tended to have high IQ's and lower scores on tests of creative thinking than over achievers.

Thorndike (1963) says that the phenomenon of under achievement and over achievement have to be interpreted in terms of artifacts of measurement and of intelligence alone.

Taylor (1964) has reported that under achievers are seen to identify themselves with a peer-group from which they always get support. He further points out that this identification with the peer-group is the outcome of the desire of the under achievers to gain some emotional security.

Taylor (1964) found that over achievers has less anxiety as compared with under achievers.

Hammel and Sprinthall (1965) in their study found that the superior achiever – in comparison with under achiever – is more mature, more thoughtful in his orientation to tasks and problems, and more willing to postpone immediate gratification to achieve distant goals. But under achievement was found to be accompanied by a number of signs of immature ego structure.

Barrett (1965) feels that under achievement results from the same cause, a feeling of insecurity and inadequacy accompanied by hostility. In another study by Barrett (1966) under achievers were found to show negativism towards school, less interest in reading, withdrawal from competition.

Matlin and Mendelssohn (1965) have found that achievement and personal adjustment are significantly correlated.

Irvine (1966) in a study concluded that male over achiever pays off more in the science area than in the other areas and science achievement causes – or is concomitant with traits, which cause – "over achievement".

In his study Sena (1966) found that over achievers are more concerned in the area of finances, living conditions and employment than under achievers, over achievers are more concerned about the future vocation and education than normal achievers. In socio-psychological area over achievers revealed more problems than either normal or under achievers.

Donald (1967) found that high school under achievers gave evidence of continued lower academic performance in college when compared with achievers. This was mostly due to factors other than academic reasons – due to home background. It was also seen that high school under achievers withdraw from college in significantly large numbers.

Joshi and Sharma (1968) found that conflicts in the family and the burden of domestic duties are important factors to under achievement.

Satyanandam (1969) has studied two sub-aspects of socio-economic status, namely educational level of parents and economic status of parents on achievement. It was found that children of graduate parents performed far better than the children of matriculate parents.

Srivasturah (1969) studied reading ability of four groups of 150 boys each representing four categories (under, over, low and high achievers). The major findings of the study were (i) in comparison with high achievers, under achievers are slow readers, and as speed and comprehension are related, they also lack the capacity to derive much meaning from what they read (ii) the under achievers had a poor stock of words and consequently and lacked the power of expression.

Vanarase (1970) investigated the possible causes for the differences in scholastic performance of normal achieving and under achieving high school students and found that the under achievers had more maladjusted parents than normal achievers. It was found that the over achievers were more self -confidence, more mature, emotionally more stable and more conscientious when compared with the under achievers.

Rao (1970) found out the relationship of intelligence, socio-economic status, study habits etc. with the scholastic achievement. He concludes that students' scholastic achievement relates more strongly to their intellectual level than to any other characteristics. There was a negative but low correlation between study habits and scholastic achievement, but a substantial positive relationship between socio-economic status and intelligence.

Bhatt's (1971) study to find out the adjustment problems of over achievers and under achievers, found that under achievers showed a better adjustment than over achievers.

Dhaliwal's (1971) study on certain factors contributing to academic success has been showed that both over and under achievement go with higher need for achievement and Greater anxiety in comparison to normal achievement is also revealed that superior study habits, reservedness, high verbal ability, emotional and social adjustment and security feelings corresponded with over achievement whereas inferior study habits, outgoing tendencies, low verbal ability, emotional instability, assertiveness, good social adjustment, were associated with academic under achievement.

Bhaduri (1971) found that over achieving students tend to be less neurotic and less anxious than under achievers. It also revealed that the under achievers tended to have a higher socio-economic status, a more congenial home condition and more of leisure time activities.

Michael (1971) attempted to find out whether educational level of parents has any effect on 'educational achievement'. The major conclusion was that the students tended to achieve and have attitudes, aspirations and expectations consistent with the educational level of their parents. The result of this study tends to support the notion that children of differently educated parents differ from children of similarly educated parents in educational achievement, attitude, aspiration and expectation.

Saxena (1972) attempted to find out the difference between over and underachievers and found that the over achievers were those who aspired to higher achievement, has sufficient endurance and possessed a capacity for fighting over their case.

Sharma (1972) compared over and under achievers with regard to their adjustment in the school, after school, self, social, home sex, health etc. The results of the study showed that over achiever had better adjustment than the under achiever. The study found that adjustment is partly dependent upon intelligence.

Sathi (1973) in her comparative study of some personality characteristics of over achievers and under achievers found that under achieving students are more extraverted than the other group.

Menon (1973) in her comparative study of the personality characteristics of over and under achievers of high ability tested the following hypothesis: 'there will be significant difference in the socio-personal characteristics motivational traits and interest patterns of over and under achieving superior ability groups. The study revealed that over achieving groups of superior and general ability is less extravert and less maladjusted than under achievers. It was found that demographic factors and socio-economic status markedly influenced over and under achievement.

Dhami (1974) in a study concluded that the effect of socio-economic status on the scholastic achievement of girls is very high. In the same study the investigator found that intelligence and emotional maturity contributed substantially to success in scholastic achievement and socio-economic status had a positive effect on emotional maturity especially the factors of parent's education family level and cultural level of the family.

John (1974) in a study to find out the interrelation between achievement motivation, test anxiety and under achievement found no significant difference for either sex with the achievement motivation but high text anxiety is significantly associated with under achieving boys.

Jayagopal's (1974) study of personality profile of under achievers revealed that they are characterized by spontaneity, vigor, spirit to associate with the group readily and uninhibited and zestful nature.

Nair (1975) and his associates studied the influence of sixteen personality variables, which are related to under achievement in mathematics among high intelligence subjects. The study found that eight adjustment variables, viz., Sense of Personal Freedom, Personal Adjustment, Test Anxiety, Withdrawing Tendencies, Nervous Symptoms, General Anxiety, Social Adjustment and Social Standards are helpful in discriminating between high-intelligence normal achievers and high-intelligence under achievers.

Mathew (1975) has attempted to identify the personality factors that cause under achievement in science. He identified the normal, under and overachievers using intelligence tests and achievement tests. He found that the mean score of normal achievers significantly exceeded the mean scores of under achievers for 'social standards'. The mean scores of over achievers significantly exceed the mean scores of under achievers in sense of personal freedom, social standards and family relations. Over achievers score less in general anxiety, test anxiety and maladjustment.

Agarwal (1975) in a study concluded that the under achievers were comparatively less emotionally mature, less calm, less prone to getting into difficulties and less able to face reality and possess less ego strength than the over achievers. The over achievers have strong educational, social and humanistic values than under achievers. The parents of over achievers gave more importance to education than the parents of under achievers.

Chaudhari (1975) made a critical study of the factors contributing to academic under achievement. According to his studies, achievement motivation of bright achievers was higher than that of bright under achievers. The study habits of achievers differ significantly from under achievers.

Studies by Mathew (1975), Iyer (1977), Abraham (1975) have shown that the number of under achievers of rural areas was greater than the number of under achievers in urban areas.

According to a study by Lalithamma (1975), children coming from large families are under achievers.

Mathew (1975) and Iyer (1977) in their studies found that there were greater incidence of under achievement among boys than girls.

Dhaliwal and Sainin (1976) studied the relationship of creativity with academic over and under achievement and found all the three components of creativity (fluency, flexibility and originality) to be positively related to intelligence.

Ghuman (1976) has studied certain affective characteristics of over achievers and under achievers and found that do not differ significantly on any of the variables viz., aptitudes, achievement, motivation and personality traits used in the study. It was also found that over achievement is primarily attributed to non-cognitive personality variables and under achievement to cognitive factors.

Beedawat (1976) found that the incidence of under achievement was higher in science group and under achievers possessed average emotional stability.

Six (1976) in a study revealed that level of anxiety is inversely a related to the complex learning demanded of a student during his initial college semester. A moderate level of anxiety appeared to be optimally conducive to over achievement in female students. Highly anxious and highly repressed male students adjusted satisfactorily.

Soman's (1977) study on secondary school children of Kerala found and test anxiety to scholastic attainment and found that low ability subjects achieve poor marks irrespective of anxiety level.

Iyer (1977) in his study found that

(i) The number of over achievers in the low age group is significantly greater than the number of over achievers in the high age group.

(ii) The number of over achieving boys significantly exceed the number of over achieving girls.

(iii) The number of over achievers in the forward caste exceeds the number of over achievers in backward caste.

(iv) There is greater incidence of over achievement among students of high parental profession than students of low parental profession.

(v) The incidence of over achievement is significantly greater among subjects whose parents have high income then among subjects who have low income.

In a study titled "Inter-personal Attitudes Associated with Under achievement of High School Pupils" Joseph (1977) found that there were greater number of under achievers among boys than among girls.

Tandon (1978) in a study of relationship between home environment and scholastic achievement of the under achievers, found that the physical, emotional and socio-economic conditions of the male group of under achievers were not wholesome. Their parents were academically less qualified, had professions which were less remunerative and had large families. The home environment was not founded to be a relevant factor in the under achievement of female under achievers.

Abraham (1978) found that higher educational level of parents is related to lower percentage of the incidence of under achievement.

Rai (1979) made comparative study of adjustment and scholastic achievement of low and high achievers. The findings were (I) high achievers differ significantly from low achievers in their adjustment (ii) there is a positive correlation between adjustment and scholastic achievement.

Nair (1979) in his attempt to compare some cognitive and affective factor structures of high and low science achievers in secondary schools found that 'low science achievers' were less anxious, both in test anxiety and general anxiety, than high science achievers.

Salunke (1979) found that though SES was unrelated to academic achievement, educational facilities and emotional happenings in home was found to contribute positively to the pupil's performance in studies.

Nagpal's (1979) study revealed that academic adjustment was an important correlate of over or under achievement. Under achievers reported a greater number of emotional problems typical to youth. The prevailing academic adjustment was an important correlate of over and under achievement. Non-intellectual factors related to acquisition of knowledge resulted in over and under achievement. Socio-economic variables related to student's determined selection but were not relevant to subsequent academic performance.

Nair (1981) has studied the role played by certain social-familial variables in causing under achievement in secondary school mathematics. The following six variables were selected for the study:

1. Father's Professional Level
2. Father's Income Level
3. Father's Education Level
4. Mother's Education Level
5. Caste
6. Family size

For the fist five variables, the critical ratios were negative which led to the conclusion, that greater incidence of under achievement is associated with the lower levels of these variables.

John and Abraham (1981) in their study identified the non-intellective variables which discriminate between achievers and under achievers as optimism – pessimism, goal perception, delayed gratification self-effort, attitude towards teachers and attitude towards academic work.

Gupta (1983) investigated that the group of low motivated over achieving boys was found to be more vigorous and zestful than the group of low motivated under achieving boys. The high motivated under achieving girls was more submissive and less tense than high motivated over achieving girls. There was significant interaction in academic achievement and achievement motivation both in case of boys as well as girls.

Reeder and Conger (1984) studied the effects of maternal and parental education, occupation and encouragement on the educational attainment of black and white women. For both groups of women, father's education was more important than that of the mother, but mother's occupation was more important than that of the father. Mothers occupation and parental expectation variables were more important for black women while parental education variables were more important for white women.

Cheriyan (1984) conducted a study of the problem faced by under achievers in secondary schools of Trivandrum city. The sample was divided into two groups viz., under achievers and non-under achievers using Farquar's regression method. The findings of the study were:

(i) there is a significant positive correlation exists between socio-economic status and academic excellence.

(ii) incidence of over achievement is 13 per cent of the total sample.

Klein's (1984) study found that very superior IQ under achievers show a greater verbal performance discrepancy and weaker ability in the 'sequencing' subtests than their achieving intellectual counterpart.

Parvathy (1984) reported significant influence of socio-familial factors such as caste affiliation, birth order, family size, socio-economic status etc. in casing under achievement in different school subjects.

Maitra (1985) has studied affective correlates of gifted under achievers. The sample of the study consisted of both gifted over achievers and under achievers. This study had concluded that the gifted over achievers are seen to be more conformist than the gifted under achievers. The under achievement seemed to be independent of the physical set up of the home or of socio-economic status in the form of their involvement in the child's activities and educational guidance.

Jagannathan (1985) found that the inter-correlation among the independent factors indicated that school environment had a positive and significant relationship with socio-economic status and home environment. The relationship of home environment with socio-economic status and school environment had a positive and significant relationship with socio-economic status and home environment with socio-economic status and school environment was significant at 5 per cent.

Natesan and Seetha (1986) in their study on achievement motivation and academic achievement concluded that there is a significant positive correlation between the variables.

Usha (1986) studied the extent of successive achievement gap (high -achievers in lower standards show a setback in their achievement in higher standards) in learning science in 416 secondary school students. She found a significant relationship between achievement gap in science and low level of aspiration of pupils.

Nair (1987) in his study titled "certain cognitive variables of creative under achievers in secondary school science" using analysis of variance found that certain cognitive variables, namely, verbal classification, proverbs total verbal intelligence, figure matrices, non-verbal intelligence: Total and 'number series' discriminate between high creative under achievers in science and low creative under achievers in science groups (boys). He also found that verbal intelligence and non-verbal intelligence discriminate the two contrasted group; namely high creative under achievers in science and low creative under achievers in science groups (girls).

Kamala (1987) in a study found that low percentage of under achievement is associated with high levels of socio-economic status.

Lower incidence of under achievement is associated with higher level of variables like SES of parents, family environment etc.

Uchat (1987) in his study has attempted to differentiate under achievers and over achievers with regard to personal factors and family factors in terms of (i) number of sibling (2) size of family (3) educational level of father (4) occupational level of father. The results showed that only age of the student significantly contributed to the phenomena of under and over achievement. The educational level of father, occupational level, size of the family etc. do not differentiate under and over achievers.

Kemmerer (1987) tried to investigate the differences between high -achieving and under achieving college freshman males and females using a 2x2 design with sex and achievement level (high vs under achievers) as the independent variables and the level of ego development, level of intellectual development as dependent variables. On level of intellectual development high -achievers scored significantly higher than under achievers and females scored significantly higher than males. In the area of identity status, high achieving males were significantly different from under achieving males for vocational identity status.

Puri (1987) in an attempt to make a detailed study of the personality traits and self-concept of under achievers found 19.8 per cent of the intellectually gifted were under achievers. The majority of under achievers belonged to lower socio-economic group and had proper self-concept. The under achiever girls tended to be more group depended and were generally tense, over- wrought and frustrated.

Flores (1989) conducted a study to investigate the effects of cross-age tutoring on under achieving fifth grade students in the areas of mathematical achievement and self-perception. A one-group pretest/ post-test design was utilized. There self-perception subscale measures were given to the under achieving fifth grade students before and after the intervention. The three self -perception subscale measures were given to the undertaking fifth grade students before and after the intervention. The three self-perception subscale measures changed significantly, but decreased overtime. The two mathematical achievement subscale measures did not change significantly overtime. These findings do not support the invention of cross- age tutoring as an effective influence on mathematical achievement or self-perception.

In a study, Jean (1989) found discrepancies mainly in general conceptions and socio-psychological factors among the four responding groups. Korean teachers and parents seemed to have a bored conception of under achievement in gifted youngsters. They tended to overlook the importance of peer relationship, psychological environment and social environments in children's achievement. Americans tended to over emphasize the psychological and social environments of under achievement. This study also revealed that study habits influence the achievement of children in positive direction.

Hishimuma (1990) in a study to identify high potential/under achiever found that total listening comprehension composite of high potential/under achiever was higher when compared to students benefiting from regular education. In the same study he found that total reading ability of high potential group performed significantly higher than high potential/under achievers and regular education samples.

Biggers (1990) investigated the effect of a multifaced theory based intrusive intervention on underachieving college freshmen. The hypotheses predicted no differences between experimental and control groups in the following areas at the conclusion of the intervention semester (a) academic performance (b) retention into the third semester of study at the same institution (c) satisfaction with various aspects of the university (d) self-reported changes in personal needs as they relate to college life. It also includes the relationship between academic achievement, retention and level of independence.

When compared to the control group the experimental group showed a better retention, a significant decline in self-reported needs and academic performance correlated positively with independence for experimental group females only, while negative correlations were found for all remaining students.

Peters (1991) conducted a study with an intention to distinguish attitude profile of gifted achievers, gifted under achievers and non-gifted students. The study found that (i) gifted achievers had significantly more positive attitudes than gifted under achievers (ii) non-gifted students had significantly more positive attitudes than gifted under achievers (iii) gifted achievers had significantly more positive attitudes than non-gifted students (iv) grade, gender and ethnicity did not significantly affect the attitudes of gifted achieving, gifted under achieving or non-gifted middle school students.

Ford (1991) conducted a study to examine the attitudes and beliefs that students hold regarding determinants of achievement. Results suggest that the majority of the students, including those identified as gifted are under achievers. Findings support the existence of a paradox of under achievement among the sample, particularly among average students and the underachievers rather than achievers. In addition, the psychological factor was found to contribute most to under achievement or lack of achievement motivation. The results also suggest that family achievement orientation plays a critical role in achievement.

Atchison (1991) analyzed the family martial status of the top versus bottom quarter of the class rank indicates that 58 per cent of students in the bottom quarter of the class came from homes where there is separation, divorce, remarriage or death of a parent. Only 19 per cent in the top quarter do not reside with both biological parents. This study also concluded that parental expectation, the nature of parental interventions, patterns of cohesion and patterns of adaptability influences the under achievers.

At the conclusion of the study, to evaluate the effectiveness of classroom activities in improving performance of the under achiever, Wilkie, *et al* (1992) have noted positive changes and substantial increases in the percent of science assignments. Significant increase in academic achievement on adult's ratings of student achievement was also noted.

Ford (1992) has studied the influences of social, psychological and cultural determinants of under achievement as perceived by 148 intermediate grade African - American students in gifted, above average, or average academic programs. Psychological factors played the greatest role in under achievement or poor achievement motivation. Under achievement behaviors were noted among students in all academic programs.

Rimm and Lovance (1992) have found that acceleration is an effective intervention in some cases of under achievement by gifted students. Lack of challenge is the primary indicator for consideration of accelerative options. Acceleration is not appropriate for all gifted students, and an adjustment period is common in successful acceleration.

Wigzell and Al-Ansari (1993) have found that the problem of failure and under achievement in foreign language learning is associated with negative attitudes and poor motivation rather than lack of aptitude.

Stipek (1993) offers guidelines to help elementary teachers motivate under achievers to work. The study recommends encouraging effort by making assigned tasks realistic, focusing students attention on their own progress, rewarding all effort, giving all students a chance to demonstrate competence in class and letting students set their own goals

Skinner (1994) in his study found that cultural influences are extremely significant in determining under achievers. He suggests that the educational community must make a greater effort to understand that LEP (Limited English Proficient) readers after being their own culturally influenced meaning to the interpretation of English language text.

Baum (1995) identified a variety of factors contributing to under achievement of high ability students, including emotional issues, social and behavioural problems, the lack of an appropriate curriculum and learning and self-regulation difficulties. The study's major finding was that almost all the students made gains in achievement, attitude or behaviour during the year of study. Several teacher behaviours emerged as crucial to student success, including

(i) taking time to get to known the student.

(ii) focusing on positive traits of the student.

(iii) understanding their role as facilitator.

(iv) applying the role of teacher as a researcher.

(v) conveying a behalf in the students' abilities.

Stein *et al* (1996) describes the problems of a child who is academically underachieving and has problem-making friends. The study emphasize the role of pediatricians in working with schools to assess children's aptitude and emotional functioning.

Grayson (1996) examined the factors contributing to under- and over- achievement in first year college students at York University on a sample of 1229 students. Majority of the students were likely to receive lower than the expected grade if they had high Ontario Academic Credit marks, were in science, believed at the beginning of the first year that family problems would interfere with their studies or were employed. Students likely to get higher than the expected grade were in environmental studies were highly involved in their classes, and earned relatively high numbers of course credits. Ford, Donna and Antoinette (1997) discusses the factor affecting the achievement of gifted minority students, problems associated with under achievement and the influence of social, cultural and psychological factors on student achievement are presented.

The study found that students favour towards varied instruction and assessment methods. Rimm (1997) has found that Under achievers generally lack internal locus of control, compete poorly and under value effort. Many under achieving children who have adopted dependent or dominant defense mechanisms can be reached using Family Achievement Clinic's Trifocal method. This multi-step process features assessment, parent- child communication, and identification of the child's profile, changing parent/ teacher expectations, and school- modification strategies.

Rivers (1998) studied the high school administrators' perceptions of under aachieving students in the low performing schools. He concluded that

(i) administrators perceived students classified as under achievers in a negative and disapproving manner.

(ii) The problems of these students aremultifaced and associated with family society as well as school conditions.

(iii) They need addressed symptoms rather than the real problem.

According to Clooney (1998) under achievement could be a attributed to a mismatch of students learning styles and teaching strategies, the student's negative relationship to learning in the past and insufficient parental support and involvement in students learning. Three strategies implemented, to strengthen the link between the teacher, students and parents, were

(i) An increased variety of teaching methods.

(ii) Students goal – setting contracts..

(iii) A home - school liaison

A study by Schultz (1999) examined how classroom climate affected the performance of gifted under achievers in a secondary science classroom. It revealed that

(i) schools exist to conform students to educational system

(ii) connections to life beyond school is lacking

(iii) curriculum needs to engage student interests

(iv) mutual respect, effort and empathy on the part of teachers and students needs to occur in the classroom

Bohannon (1999) sought to determine the impact of school related stresses to discipline referrals, attendance, grade point average and under achievement among High School students. In all the four cases the composite correlations were found to be significant.

A qualitative study by Sharif (1999) revealed that parent intervention programmes, family literacy programmes, cultural awareness programmes and critical multicultural educational programmes are needed for systematic change to occur among under achievers.

Khan (1999) found that verbal praise by the classroom teacher increased student (under achiever) discourse in the classroom.

Davis (1999) concluded in his study that genetic and environmental factors influence one's observable characteristics. The achieving and under achieving gifted children were discriminated when selected psychological and demographic characteristics are taken as predictor variables.

Rhoad (1999) studied the factors related to under achieving students. Low income, teacher behaviour, parental involvement and class/school size are significant factors for under achievement.

CHAPTER 4

METHODOLOGY

This chapter summarises the details relating to the design of the study, classified under the following heads:

A. Variables of the study

B. Hypotheses

C. Methodology

A. VARIABLES OF THE STUDY

The major focus of the study, as explained in earlier sections of this report, is to identify a select set of psychological and familial variables, which can be used to discriminate between Discrepant Achievers and Non Discrepant Achievers in different school subjects, namely, Malayalam, English, Hindi, Social Studies, Science and Mathematics. This objective involved the following steps:

1. To identify (making use of the information available in published literature and classroom / practical observations) a group of psychological and familial variables that are associated with Discrepant and Non Discrepant Achievers in various school subjects.

2. To find out which of the variables identified as above will discriminate between Discrepant Achievers and Non Discrepant Achievers in different school subjects in a population of secondary school pupils of Kerala.

The first task was the selection of the independent variables for the study. The criteria to be used for selecting the independent variables were spelt out. Theoretical and practical considerations led to the formulation of the following criteria for selecting the independent variables:

(i) the selected variables should to the extent possible represent a wide variety of psychological and familial functions which are capable of being measured with sufficient degree of accuracy and practicability.

(ii) the selected variables should be such as would show relationship with Discrepant Achievers and Non Discrepant Achievers in different school subjects.

(iii) the selected variables should represent abilities or traits which are not directly developed through schooling, but are developed through the influence of the socio-cultural environment.

(iv) taking into consideration the context in which the study is to be extended, the selected variables should be such as would render themselves to measurement through group tests administered.

The above criteria were used by the investigator for selecting different psychological and familial variables for the study. Accordingly the following variables were used in the design of the present study:

(a) Independent Variables

Seven psychological variables and five familial variables have been used as the independent variables of the study. They are:

Psychological Variables

a. Personal Adjustment

b. Social Adjustment

c. General Anxiety

d. Examination Anxiety

e. Introversion – extraversion

f. Masculinity – femininity

g. Achievement Motivation

Familial Variables

1. Family Education Level
2. Family Cultural Level.
3. Family Environment.
4. Family Acceptance.
5. Home Learning Facility.

(b) Classificatory Variables

The following variables are used for the purpose of classification of students into different categories namely, discrepant achievers and non- discrepant achievers:

1. Achievement in six school subjects (Malayalam, English, Hindi, Social Studies, Science and Mathematics)
2. Intelligence (Verbal and Non- verbal)

B. HYPOTHESES

The study has been designed around the major hypothesis that each of the independent variables selected for study will discriminate significantly between the Discrepant Achievers and Non Discrepant Achievers in various school subjects.

The following sub hypotheses were deduced from the major hypotheses presented earlier:

(a) each of the Psychological - Familial variables selected for study will discriminate significantly between Discrepant and Non Discrepant Achievers in Malayalam.

(b) each of the Psychological - Familial variables selected for study will discriminate significantly between Discrepant and Non Discrepant Achievers in English.

(c) each of the Psychological - Familial variables selected for study will discriminate significantly between Discrepant and Non Discrepant Achievers in Hindi.

(d) each of the Psychological - Familial variables selected for study will discriminate significantly between Discrepant and Non Discrepant Achievers in Social Studies.

(e) each of the Psychological - Familial variables selected for study will discriminate significantly between Discrepant and Non Discrepant Achievers in Science.

(f) each of the Psychological - Familial variables selected for study will discriminate significantly between Discrepant and Non Discrepant Achievers in Mathematics.

C. METHODOLOGY

The important details relating to the methodology adopted for the study are described below under the following major heads:

(i) Tools used for measurement

(ii) Sample used for the study

(iii) Data collection procedures

(iv) Scoring and consolidation of data

(v) Statistical techniques used for analysis

Each of these is described below:

1. Tools used for Measurement

A number of standardized psychological and educational tests were used for measuring the different variables. The details of the tools used in the study are presented in Table 1.

Table 1 : Details of the Tools used for the study

	Name of the Tools	Variable Measured
	1	2
1.	Kerala University Group Testof Intelligence (Verbal)	Verbal Intelligence: (Total)
2.	The Kerala Non - verbal Group Test of Intelligence for Secondary Schools	Non -verbal Intelligence: Total
3.	Kerala Socio – personal Adjustment Scale	Social Adjustment and Personal Adjustment
4.	Kerala Examination Anxiety Scale	Examination Anxiety
5.	Kerala General Anxiety Scale	General Anxiety
6.	The Kerala Introversion - extraversion Scale	Introversion – extraversion
7.	The Kerala Masculinity - femininity Scale	Masculinity – femininity
8.	Kerala Scale of Achievement Motivation	Achievement Motivation
9.	Family Cultural Level Rating Scale	Family Cultural Level
10	Family Environment Index Inventory	Family Environment
11	Family Acceptance of Education Rating Scale	Family Acceptance of Education
12	Home Learning Facility Inventory	Home Learning Facility

1	2
13 General Achievement Tests for Standard IX	Achievement in Malayalam Achievement in English Achievement in Hindi Achievement in Social Studies Achievement in General Science Achievement in Mathematics
14 Kerala Socio Economic Scale	Family Education Level

The psychometric descriptions and other relevant details of the different tests used in the study are presented below:

(i) Kerala University Group Test of Intelligence (Verbal)

This is a point scale of intelligence in Malayalam developed for measuring the general intelligence of pupils in secondary schools of Kerala. This has been developed by Pillai , Nair and Amma (1968). It is composed of five sub-tests as detailed in Table 2.

Table 2 : Sub-Tests, Number of Items and the Time limit for each Sub-Test in the Verbal Group Test of Intelligence

Sub – tests	No. of Items	Time Limit
Verbal Analogy	20	5 minutes
Verbal Classification	20	5 minutes
Proverbs	20	5 minutes
Number Series	20	10 minutes
Verbal Reasoning	20	8 minutes

The nature of the sub - tests is described below:

I. ***Verbal Analogy*** : In each problem three words are given of which the first two words suggest a relationship. A missing fourth word has to be found out from the given relationship. The relationship holding between the first two words has to be identified and used to find the fourth word. The answer is to be selected from the four words given in brackets. Examples of the items in this sub-tests are given below :

1. Train : Station Ship : ————

 (a. Sea b. Lake c. Harbor d. Boat)

2. Policeman :Hat King : ————

 (a. Throne b. Crown c. Kingdom d. Palace)

This test includes 20 items and the time limit is 5 minutes. It involves the ability to see the relationship between two things or ideas and to use the relationship to other situations. The items are based on Spearman's principle of cognition given below:

1. A person tend to find relations between the parts of any apprehended material

2. If a presentation is apprehended by a person and a relationship presented with it, the related experience or concept (correlate) is also evoked. Factor analytic studies showed that this involves a reasoning factor identified as 'eduction of relationships'.

II. Verbal Classification

In each item five words are given of which four can be grouped together according to some principles or law. The pupil has to choose the word that does not fit in the class of other words, and mark it in the score card according to instruction given :

1. (a) Addition (b) Subtraction

 (c) Multiplication (d) Arithmetic

 (e) Division

2. (a) Football (b) Cricket

(c) Hockey (d) Chess

(e) Volleyball

Twenty items are included in the test. The mental process involved in answering items of this type is identified to be the same as that in analogy i.e., the mental process involved is 'eduction of relationships'.

III. Proverbs

Each item consists of a proverb followed by four statements explaining its meaning. The pupils have to choose the statement, which comes very close to the idea contained in the proverb. Two examples from the test are given below:

1. Slow and steady wins the race

   (a) If we eat slowly we can eat a large amount of food

   (b) If we do slowly we can finish a work however hard it may be

   (c) Any work should be done slowly

   (d) Any work which is done slowly is good

2. All that glitters is not gold

   (a) External and internal characters are not the same

   (b) All shining things are not gold

   (c) Gold need not glitter always

   (d) Don't be amazed by seeing the outward appearance

There are twenty items in the test. Items of this type are mostly saturated with 'g' factor of intelligence (Anastasi,1962). The mental ability involved in selecting the best statement is supposed to be "verbal comprehension".

IV. Number series

In each item a series of numbers in a certain order is given of which one is missing. The pupils have to choose the correct number from those given in brackets. Two illustrative examples are given below:

1. 5, 9, 13,17, 21,...... (a. 25 b. 34 c. 17)

2. 3/4 , 4/5, 5/6, 6/7, 7/8, (a. 7/16, b. 8/9 c.18)

This sub-test consists of 20 items. Thurstone identified that the mental ability involved in this type of problems is 'inductive reasoning' (Grune,1952)

V. Verbal Reasoning

A problem requiring the perception of some sort of relationship and its identification is given. The pupils have to select the correct answer to the problem from the four alternatives given. Two illustrative examples are as follows:

1. Suma is older than Usha. Geetha is younger than Usha. Prema is older than Suma. Then who is the oldest of them.

   a. Suma b. Usha c. Geetha d. Prema

2. A family went out for a walk. Son walked before the father. Daughter was walking behind the father and ahead of mother. Who walked last?

   a. Father b. Mother c. Son d. Daughter

Twenty problems of the above sort are included in sub-test. Thurstone identified that the mental ability involved in answering items of this type is 'deductive reasoning' (Nunnally ,1959).

Validity and Reliability

The test components have been adopted from popular standardised test with high 'g' loadings. This has been followed by procedures for attaining high internal validity ensured through item analysis. Inter- test correlation of the sub - tests has been worked out on a select representative sample (N=120). The inter-test correlations of the five tests in the battery are given in Table.3.

TABLE 3 : INTER -TEST CORRELATION MATRIX OF THE SUB- TESTS OF THE VERBAL GROUP TEST OF INTELLIGENCE.

	Sub-tests	1	2	3	4	5
1.	Verbal Analogy		.75	.66	.45	.56
2.	Verbal Classification			.63	.47	.41
3.	Proverbs				.47	.41
4.	Number Series					.32
5.	Verbal Reasoning					..

External validity was calculated against school marks (N = 50) and against Raven's Progressive Matrices Test (N = 120). These were found to be 0.64 and 0.56 respectively.

The factorial validity of the test was later determined by Kurup (1969). This study shows that 79 per cent of the common variance of the battery was accounted for by a general factor, the 'g' factor of intelligence.

The test retest reliability on a sample of 86 was 0.79. The split half reliability of the whole test and sub - tests (N = 120) is given in Table 4.

TABLE 4: SPLIT - HALF RELIABILITY OF THE VERBAL GROUP TEST OF INTELLIGENCE

	Sub – tests	Reliability Coefficient
1.	Verbal Analogy	0.88
2.	Verbal Classification	0.86
3.	Proverbs	0.86
4.	Number Series	0.86
5.	Verbal Reasoning	0.84

The values and procedures cited above show that the test is a valid and reliable measure of 'g' factor of intelligence.

(ii) The Kerala Non-Verbal Group Test of Intelligence for Secondary Schools

This is a popular non-verbal test of intelligence standardized by Nair (1968) for use with Kerala secondary school children. The test consists of four sub-tests. The details of the components, the number of items in each and time allotted for each sub-test are given in Table 5.

TABLE 5 : SUB - TESTS OF THE KERALA NON- VERBAL GROUP TEST OF INTELLIGENCE.

	Sub – tests	Number of Items	Time in Minutes
1.	Figure Classification	20	5
2.	Figure Series	20	5
3.	Figure Analogies	20	5
4.	Figure Matrices	20	5

Description of the sub - tests

*1. **Figure Classification*** : Each of the 20 items consists of five abstract figures, four of which belong to the same group on the basis of some order, rule, principle, but one figure will stand out as not belonging to the group. The pupils have to identify the figure which does not go into the group. The answer has to be selected from a list of five abstract figures given. Examples are given below :

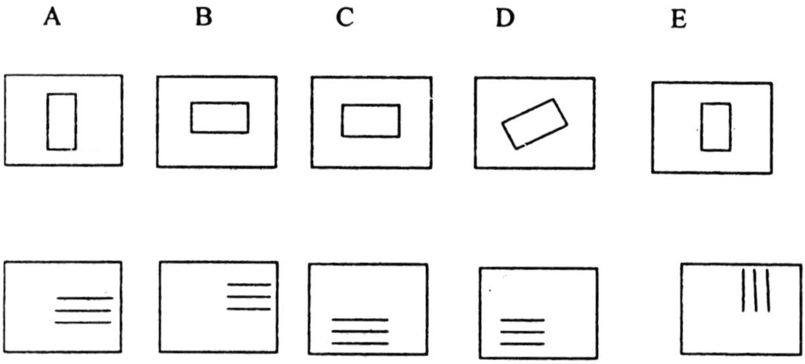

*2. **Figure Series*** : Each item in this sub-test contains a sequence of five abstract figures. The first four figures have been formed according to a certain rule or principle. The fifth missing figure has to be identified by the pupils, from a given set of four alternative abstract figures. An illustrative example is given below:

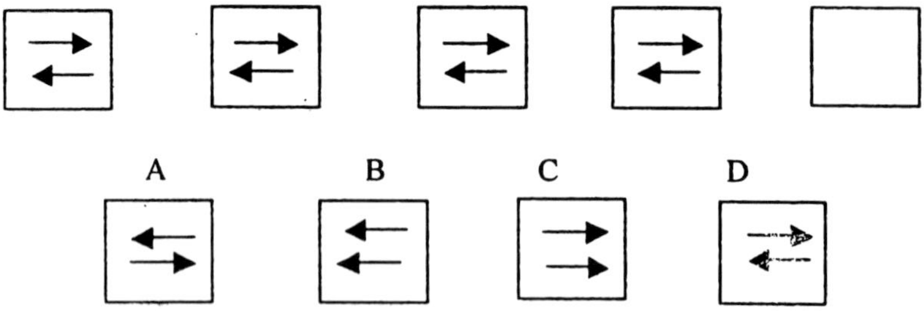

*3. **Figure Analogies*** : Each item in this subtest contains three abstract figures of which the first two figures are related to each other in a particular way. Applying the relationship that exist between the first two figures, the pupils have to find out the fourth figure (from among the four alternatives given) so that the third and fourth figures bear the same relationship as the one between the first and the second. An illustrative example is given below:

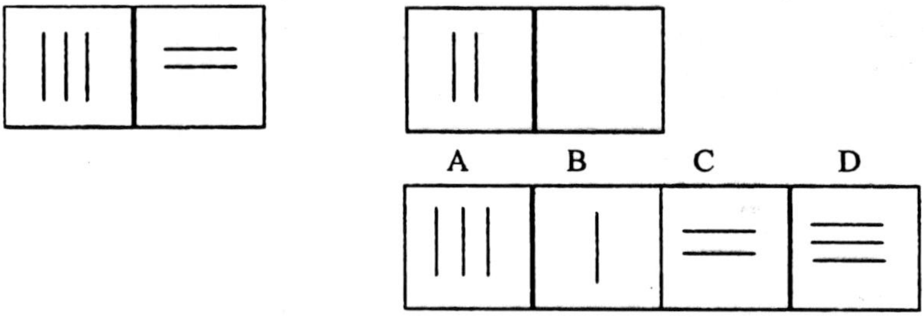

4. ***Figure Matrices*** : This contains nine abstract figures arranged in three rows and three columns. The right hand bottom figure is missing. By examining the first two rows or columns, the pupils have to discover the principle which connect the figures in the first two rows or columns and then use the relationship to find out the missing figure. An example is given below :

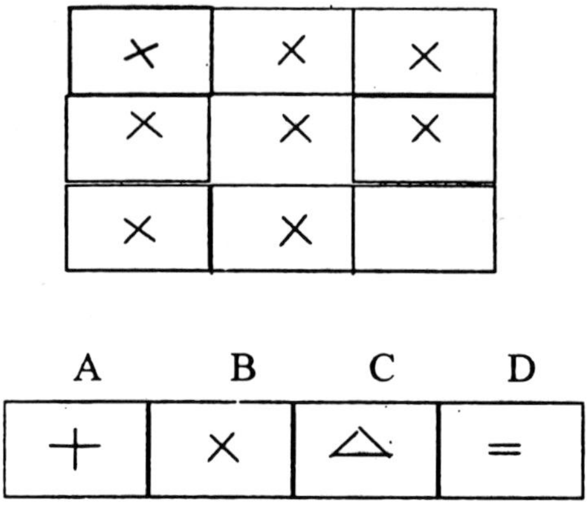

Validity and Reliability

The validity of the test has been established using different tests as external criterion. The test manual provides data regarding the validity of the tests. The following correlations have been reported for the external criteria noted below:

With Raven's P.M.T	r = 0.784	(N = 256)
With Kerala University Group Test of		
Intelligence (Verbal)	r = 0.734	(N = 256)
With Teacher's Rating	r = 0.520	(N = 504)
With Total School Marks	r = 0.537	(N = 324)

Factor analysis of the battery with the PMT and Kerala University Group Test of Intelligence (Verbal) as reference tests revealed the presence of a major factor in all the tests of the battery which is a close approximation to Spearman's 'g' factor of intelligence. Another less important common factor, a space perception factor, was also detected.

The test retest reliability coefficient of the test has been calculated for different intervals. For a three months interval, the reliability was 0.76 (N=246) for a one month interval, the reliability was 0.75 (N=124) and for a one week interval reliability was 0.8 (N=121).

Corrected split–half coefficients of reliability for the whole test battery and for the component tests (N= 237) are given in Table 6.

TABLE 6 : SPLIT-HALF RELIABILITY COEFFI-CIENTS FOR THE KERALA NON - VERBAL GROUP TEST OF INTELLIGENCE

	Sub - tests	Split – half Reliability Coefficients
1	Figure Classification	0.92
2.	Figure Series	0.90
3.	Figure Analogies	0.88
4	Figure Matrices	0.88
	Whole test	**0.91**

The use of Rational Equivalence method gave a reliability of 0.84 (N = 100) for the whole test.

The validity and reliability data show that the test is both a valid and reliable tool for measuring intelligence of secondary school students of Kerala.

(iii) Kerala Socio-Personal Adjustment Scale (Revised Version)

This is a test modeled after the California Test of Personality and standardised for use with secondary school students of Kerala. The test is in Malayalam. This was prepared by Nair (1970). This is a modified and revised version of The Kerala University Socio-personal Adjustment Scale. The original scale after which the present scale is modified, viz; the California Test of Personality is organized around the concept of 'life adjustment', which is considered to be a balance between 'Personal' and 'Social' Adjustment. This broad two-fold division is consistent with the common practice of classifying adjustment difficulties in to 'personality problems' (Personal Adjustment) and 'conduct problems' (Social Adjustment).

The battery as a whole may be considered to be a measure of Socio -Personal Adjustment.

Description of the Test

The battery of tests consists of twelve sub-tests divided into 2 sets of six each; the first set measures 'Personal Adjustment' while the second set measures 'Social Adjustment'.

The Personal Adjustment scale includes sub-tests 1 to 6 marked IA, IB, IC, ID,IE and IF.

The variables which can be measured are the following:

IA Self Reliance

IB Sense of Personal Worth

IC Sense of Personal Freedom

ID Feeling of Belonging

IE Withdrawing Tendencies (freedom from)

IF Nervous Symptoms (freedom from)

The second set for measuring 'Social Adjustment' consists of six subtests.

These sub-tests are the following :

IIA Social Standards

IIB Social Skills

IIC Anti-social Tendencies (freedom from)

IID Family Relations

IIE School Relations

IIF Community Relations

I. Personal Adjustment

Description of the sub - tests.

***I A.* Self Reliance**

It has been found that those who depend on themselves in various situations are generally responsible and emotionally stable. Self-reliance forms a part of personal adjustment because self-reliant persons are confident of their dealing with others and their personal problems are solved by themselves. In most of the known adjustments inventories, self-reliance is included as a trait that promotes general adjustment.

Examples of items in these sub-tests are :

1. Do you usually finish the job that you have started?

2. Do you seek the help of elder boys in the class for talking to unkind teachers?

I B. Sense of Personal Worth

Even though this is included in personal adjustment it definitely has a social reference, for only in a social context can an individual assess his own worth. The person having a sense of personal worth feels that he is well regarded by others and hence feels capable and confident. Items in this sub-test include:

1. Do you think that your classmates like your being in the class ?

2. Do you think that your parents and teachers are doubtful of your abilities ?

I C. Sense of Personal Freedom

Children, especially in their adolescent age want some freedom like freedom to choose friends, to have some money to be spent etc. The thwarting of these wishes lead to frustration and consequent maladjustment. An individual enjoys a sense of freedom when he is permitted to have a reasonable share in the determination of his conduct and in setting the general policies that shall govern his life.

Examples of items in this category are :

1. Do elders blame you for even silly matters ?

2. Do you feel that others interfere in your matters?

I D. Feeling of Belonging :

Researchers prove that social acceptance is a crucial factor for healthy mental development when an individual has a feeling of belonging, his needs for love and recognition are satisfied. He can enjoy the cordial relationship with people in general:

Two of the items in this sub - test are :

1. Do you find it difficult to make friends with new classmates?

2. Have you felt that others treat you without understanding your abilities?

I E. Withdrawing Tendencies (freedom from)

It is wrong to conclude that those who rebel alone are maladjusted pupils. Serious forms of maladjustment are seen in pupils who are extremely quiet. Causes like frustration of needs or inferiority complex may result in withdrawing tendencies. Such students find enjoyment only in fantasy and these prevent the student from mingling with others. Examples of items in this sub - test are:

1. Do you feel that you have more problem than other boys like you?

2. When lessons are going on in the class, do you think of something more important than the lessons?

I F. Nervous Symptoms (freedom from)

This is comparatively more common form of maladjustment seen in classroom situations and it affects the performance of the students seriously. This type of maladjustment is depicted in various physical symptoms like sneezing frequently, nail biting, frequent eyestrain or headache, tendency to be chronically tired etc.

Items in this sub - test include the following:

1. Are you often unable to do things properly because of headache?

2. While studying do you feel tired often?

II. Social Adjustment

II A. Social Standards

Social standards may vary from culture to culture, and they assume a deciding role in the individuals behaviour and in his social adjustment.

Examples of items in this sub - test are:

1. Do you think that it is necessary to be courteous to those whom you do not like?

2. While traveling by bus or train is it wrong if you take a little more space than what is required to sit ?

II B. Social Skills

In addition to knowing the norms of society an individual needs certain social skills which enable him to put this knowledge effectively into practice. Observation of overt behaviour can also be used to assess the social skills, which vary with age, sex, occupation, social status etc. The items in this category include:

1. Have you found it difficult to congratulate others when they succeed?

2. Do you find it difficult to address the class because others watch you?

II C. Anti-social Tendencies (freedom from)

This form of maladjustment may arise because of reasons that pertain to the individual also. The most obvious form of maladjustment is seen in anti-social tendencies. The anti-social individual finds satisfaction of his needs in ways that are disturbing and unfair to others. Examples of items of this sub - test are:

1. Have you found that lying is the easiest way to escape from difficulties?

2. Do you wish to disturb others when they do not listen to what you say?

II D. Family Relations

Family relations assume very great significance in the adjustment process. Satisfaction of the need for love and security and the consequent emergency of self respect depend greatly upon good family relations. Parental control is a potent factor in the social adjustment of students in secondary schools. Items in this subtest include:

1. Do you often quarrel with others at home ?

2. Do you often feel that nobody at home cares for you ?

II E. School Relations

School comes next to the family in its influence on behaviour. In school, the student learns lessons of group life and co-operation, that are most essential for satisfactory social adjustment. The student who has satisfactory school relations feels that he is loved by students and teachers. He finds the school work adopted to his level of ability and interest:

Two of the items in this sub - test are :

1. Do You think that some of the school subjects are very difficult ?

2. Do you feel that teachers behave more harshly than is needed?

II F. Community Relations

Good adjustment with the community depends much on factors like learning, maturity, social status, occupation etc. Those with good community relations tend to be mingling freely and happily with their neighbours. They show tolerance to strangers and are generally respectful of laws and regulations.

Examples of items in this sub - test are :

1. Do you think that you like most of your neighbours?

2. Do you think that your neighbours consider you as a relative?

Administration and scoring

The overall time for administration of the battery is approximately fifty minutes. Each of the 12 sub-tests consists of 15 items. The items are in the form of questions each of which is to be responded by marking against 'Yes' or 'No'.

Validity and Reliability

The present test is a standardised test of personality constructed on the theoretical model of the California Test of Personality. Evidence regarding the validity and reliability of the scale is available in the test manual and in a number of other studies. The scale claims its validity mainly on the basis of the manner in which it was constructed. This tool has taken its content from the California Test of Personality. Its rightly claims its content validity.

The validity of this scale is claimed mostly on the basis of the psychometric procedures used and the psychological model used for developing the scale. The total score on the scale was compared against another scale of adjustment in use in Kerala - the adaptations of the Personal Adjustment Inventory – and the score correlated 0.63 with the 'Emotional Stability' component of that scale. The total scores also correlated 0.62 with the 'Personal Relations' component of the same scale. A factor analytic study of the earlier version of this scale by Remadevi (1971) showed that the scale is basically a measure of a single personality factor, viz., 'Socio- Personal Adjustment'.

The test-retest reliability coefficients obtained by one researcher (Nair,1975) on a sample of 100 with an interval of two weeks varies from 0.69 to 0.82. The reliability coefficient obtained by another researcher Babu (1977) on a sample of 96 subjects with an interval of about one month between the two testing vary from 0.71 to 0.83. The obtained reliability coefficients of the sub-tests are presented in Table-7.

TABLE 7 : RELIABILITY COEFFICIENTS OF THE 12 SUB - TESTS AND THE WHOLE TEST OF THE PERSONALITY SCALE

	Sub-tests	Reliability Coefficients
1.	Self Reliance	0.76
2.	Sense of Personal Worth	0.76
3.	Sense of Personal Freedom	0.76
4.	Feeling of Belonging	0.83
5.	Withdrawing Tendencies (freedom from)	0.80
6.	Nervous Symptoms (freedom from)	0.79
7.	Social Standards	0.75
8.	Social Skills	0.71
9.	Anti-social Tendencies (freedom from)	0.77
10.	Family Relations	0.81
11.	School Relations	0.81
12.	Community Relations	0.82
	Whole Test	**0.79**

On the basis of these evidences, the scale may be taken to be reasonably valid and reliable measure of the two adjustment components selected for the study.

(iv) Kerala Examination Anxiety Scale

This test consists of 30 simple questions to be answered by choosing any one of the following alternatives. 'Y' (Yes) 'U' (undecided) and 'N' (No). Among the 30 items for four items the correct response is 'Yes' and for the rest 26 items the correct response is 'No'. Each correct response is given one mark. There is no time limit. This scale is in Malayalam and English and has been standardized for use with Kerala secondary school subjects with empirically selected components for indicating test anxious behaviour under Kerala conditions. This scale is popular measure of 'examination anxiety' used by several social and educational researchers in Kerala. This test was prepared by Nair (1978).

Specimen items of this test are given below:

1. I don't like teachers who give frequent class tests
2. My vision gets blurred while I try to read the question paper for the first time.

Validity and Reliability

This test has been developed on the broad model of the well-known PAT Anxiety Scale. Evidence regarding the scale's validity is provided in terms of the theoretical model implied in the development of the scale. Other evidence is provided by an independent study conducted by Mathew (1975) with achievement (r = -0. 203) and intelligence (r = -0.289) for a sample of 727 secondary school pupils. The same study also reveals that this test has high positive correlation with general anxiety (r = 0. 605).

The reliability of the test has been worked out in another study by Babu (1977) using the test-retest method. The study indicates that the test has a test- retest reliability of 0.79. The available evidence shows that this test is a valid and reliable measure of 'Examination Anxiety' as applied to secondary school pupils of Kerala.

(v) Kerala General Anxiety Scale

The Kerala General Anxiety Scale by Nair (1976) has been modeled on the well known IPAT Anxiety Scale and standardized for use with secondary school pupils of Kerala. This test consists of 32 items. The subjects are expected to respond to each statement by choosing any one of the following alternatives: 'Y' (Yes), 'U' (Undecided) and 'N' (No) on the score sheet provided. No time limit is imposed on the test. A score of one is given for each 'Y' response and zero for the other two responses. Specimen items are given below :

1. The thought that others have a low estimate of me does not disturb my peace of mind.

2. I am easily disturbed during rainy days at the thought that my house will be hit by thunder and lightning.

Validity and reliability

Evidence regarding the scale's validity is provided in terms of the theoretical model implied in the original model, viz., the IPAT scale. Other evidence is provided by independent researchers. The study by Mathew (1972) for example, showed that the test correlates negatively with both achievement (r = -0.183) and intelligence (r = -0.204) for a sample of 727 secondary school pupils. The same study shows that the test correlates positively with Test Anxiety (r = 0.605).

The reliability of the test has been worked out in another study by Samuel (1972). The study showed that the test - retest reliability of the test is 0.78. The split - half reliability of the test was found to be 0.82. The available evidences, thus, show that this tool is a reasonably valid and reliable measure of 'general anxiety' of secondary school pupils of Kerala.

(vi) The Kerala Introversion-extraversion Scale

The psychological dimension which is described as 'introversion –extraversion, was prepared by Nair (1979) for use with the secondary school pupils of Kerala. There are thirty statements in the scale developed on the models of the well - known scales like the Freud - Heidbreder's Introversion -extraversion test, the Bernreuter Personality Inventory, Myers- Briggs Type Indicator, etc. The pupils have to respond to each of these statements by choosing any one of the following alternatives: 'A' (Agree), 'U' (Undecided) and 'D' (Disagree). The scale can be scored both for introversion and extraversion, using different keys. Extraverted behaviour is measured through the presence of symptoms like interest in overt activity, mental disconcertedness, happy - go - lucky disposition and impulsive reactions. The introverted dimension is measured through behavior symptoms indicating thinking introversion reflectiveness, observant nature, meditativeness and philosophically inclined, being possessed and serious minded, persistence and ability to control oneself. Out of the thirty items, fifteen items indicate extraverted behavior while the remaining are symptomatic of introversion. Both types of items are scored in reverse directions. When the scoring is for introversion, positive scoring is given for an 'Agree' response to an extraversion item. The scale was scored for introversion in the present case. This is the score in the test, as used in the study, could be treated as an introversion score.

Some representative items of the scale are given below :

1. Very often you find yourself acting before thinking about what you are doing.

2. You like to evaluate your past actions carefully.

Validity and reliability

The validity of the scale, again reported in the test manual, has been estimated against the extraversion scale of Bernreuter Personality Inventory. The introversion score obtained from an English medium class division (N = 55) was used as the external criterion for validity of the present test. The resulting correlation was as high as 0.73. The choice of items (adapted for Indian culture) from the well - known clinical scales measuring introversion - extraversion may be taken as additional proof of the validity of the scale.

The reliability of the scale (as reported in the manual) has been established by split - half method and test-retest method. The split-half reliability coefficient for the scale is 0.82 (N = 75)for the whole test. The scale has test - retest reliability coefficient of 0.81 (N = 105) when the two testing were separated by an one-month interval.

The particulars presented above indicate that the scale is a reasonably valid and reliable tool for measuring the 'Introversion-extraversion' dimension of personality of the secondary school pupils of Kerala.

(vii) The Kerala Masculinity-femininity Scale

This is a standardised scale developed by Nair (1979) for use with senior secondary school pupils of Kerala. The scale has been widely used by researchers in Kerala. There are thirty items in the scale in the form of statements. The scale helps to measure both masculine and feminine traits, depending upon the scoring scheme adapted. In the present study the scoring has been done for 'masculinity'. Hence the score obtained may be treated as the 'masculinity score' of the subjects. The scale measures aspects like emotions and interests, activity, preferences, mode of reacting to familiar situations, methods of expressing emotional reactions to situations etc. For each statement the pupils are required to respond by selecting any of the three responses 'A' (Agree) 'U' (Undecided) and 'D' (Disagree). When scoring is for masculinity, positive scoring (+1) is given for an A response and a negative scoring (-1) is given for an A response in the feminine form. There is no time limit for the test.

The representative items are presented below:

(i) You don't mind sitting in a room full of disarranged things.

(ii) When you become emotional, you come to the point of tears.

Validity and Reliability

The evidence regarding to the validity of the test is provided in terms of construct validity and the result of experimental assessments. The scale possesses a reasonable degree of construct validity, since the items have been prepared using items (or adaptation thereof) used in established scales and the theoretical basis used for constructing the scales. The concurrent validity of the scale has been established by correlating the masculinity scores of the scale with an adapted version of the masculinity scale of the Guilford-Zimmerman-Temperament Survey. The correlation was as high as 0.66 (N=85) for a group of college students.

The reliability of the scale as reported in the test manual (scored for masculinity) has been estimated in two different ways viz., test retest method and split-half method. The test retest reliability coefficient of the scale worked out in a sample of 115 senior secondary school pupils (3 weeks test - retest interval) is reported to be 0.83. The correlated split-half reliability coefficient of the scale obtained on a sample of 100 university entrants is 0.88.

There psychometric properties show that the scale is a valid and reliable tool for measuring the masculinity-femininity dimension of personality of the secondary school pupils of Kerala.

(viii) Kerala Scale of Achievement Motivation

The scale developed by Nair (1976) has 60 items in the form of statements and is standardised to measure the level of Achievement Motivation among secondary school pupils of Kerala.

The subjects are to respond to the items by marking either 'Y' (Yes) 'U" (Undecided) or 'N' (No) on the response sheet supplied . Each 'Y' response carries one credit. There is no time limit for the test.

Two illustrative items are :

1. Many people consider that I am one who cannot do anything useful or worthwhile.

2. I will never be satisfied with my present achievement; I would like to do something more important in my life.

There are both positive items (items showing high achievement motivation) and negative items (items showing lack of achievement motivation) in the test. A mark under 'Y' will be given a unit score for a positive item while a mark under 'N' will receive a unit score for a negative item. All other responses will receive zero scores. The total scores on the test is the sum of the scorers obtained by a pupil in all the items of the test.

(ix) Family Cultural Level Rating Scale

This is an eighteen-item rating scale for measuring the cultural level of a family. The subjects are expected to respond to each item using a three point scale. The test has been developed by Nair and Devi (1981). The test items relate to different aspects of domestic life and social behaviour of the members of a family, which vary from the number of newspapers and magazines bought, to how the parents correct their children when they behave in a crude manner towards others. Two representative items of this scale are given below:

(i)	The number of cultural organization in which you (other members of your family) are members .	Many ( )	Few ( )	None ( )
(ii)	Your parents encourage you to listen to all the educational broadcast.	Always ( )	Sometimes ( )	Never ( )

Response is to be made by ticking in the appropriate space. Tick mark in the lowest point of the scale would receive a unit score, scoring in the next two points would be allocated scores of two and three respectively. The score for each subject is the sum of the scores obtained by the individual for all the items.

Validity and Reliability

The validity and reliability of the test is reported in the test manual. The test has been validated by correlating it with the Kerala Socio-economic Scale for a sample of secondary school pupils. The coefficient of correlation is 0.38 (N = 47). The split-half reliability of the test was estimated in a sample of 84 school pupils. The test indicated a relatively high degree of reliability (0.83). The validity and reliability indices show that the test is a reasonably good instrument for measuring the construct in question.

(x) Family Environment Index Inventory

This is a popular research tool for measuring 'family environment'. This inventory has been developed by Nair and Devi (1981) for the use of social researchers who want to obtain a quick index of the family environment, in terms of its cultural and social advancement. The test is in the form of a rating scale with fourteen items. The response to each item is to be made by entering a tick mark against it in one of the three rating scale points. Two representative items are given below:

		Many	Few	One
(i)	The number of huge buildings in the vicinity of your home	( )	( )	( )
(ii)	The frequency of quarrels among your neighbours.	( )	( )	( )

The subject is required to put a tick mark in one of the three brackets given against each positive items (showing socially accepted and therefore better environment) and are scored by assigning scores 1,2 or 3 to tick marks 'none', 'few' or 'many' respectively. Negative items (showing the absence of factors indicating cultural level) will be scored in the reverse order. The score in the inventory is the sum total of the scores assigned to an individual for all the fourteen items.

Validity and Reliability

The scale has been validated against rating by specialists. Forty-five households occupied by forty-five respondents were independently rated by a team of three social researchers. They rated the family environment by observing the surroundings and rating each on a five point scale. The ratings were converted into scores using conventional procedures. The scores assigned by the three members were arranged and used as the external criterion. A product moment correlation of 0.47 was obtained showing that the scale is a reasonably valid instrument for measuring 'family environment'. The split-half reliability (N = 79) was 0.66, again showing that it is a reasonably reliable instrument.

(xi) Family Acceptance of Education Rating Scale

This is a popular scale for measuring the construct of 'family acceptance of education' with particular reference to Kerala. This scale has been developed by Nair and Devi (1981). The construct is measured with the help of sixteen items to which the subjects have to respond, with the help of a three point scale. Some representative items of the scale are given below :

		Always	Sometimes	Never
(i)	Your parents help you to learn difficult subjects.	( )	( )	( )
(ii)	Your parents buy you popular books which will enrich your learning.	( )	( )	( )

'Never' response is given a zero score; the 'sometimes' response is given a 'unit' score while the 'always' response would receive a score, 'two'. The score of a subject is the sum of the scores obtained by a respondent for all the sixteen items of the scale.

Validity and Reliability

The authors of the scale claim validity in terms of the procedure adopted for developing the scale, and in terms of the results of the external validation study conducted by them. A part, from the fact that the sixteen items has been selected by a select panel of 20 judges from a list of 100 items presented to them, the test has been validated against two external criteria. The coefficient of correlation of the scores on the rating scale with total class achievement (marks obtained by pupils in a generalised achievement test in six school subjects is 0.39. The study used 123 pupils of standard X. Another validity study used the same sample. The scores of the scale were correlated with the scores on another standardised scale viz., 'Scale of Attitude Towards Academic work'. The correlation in this case was 0.44. The split-half reliability of the scale using a sub- sample (N=54) of the above sample was estimated as 0.73. These values show that the scale is a reasonably valid and reliable instrument for the purpose of the present study.

(xii) Home Learning Facility Inventory

This is an eighteen item inventory developed by Nair and Devi (1981). This inventory consists of three sections, each containing a list of six basic facilities required for home learning. These vary from, whether there is a separate table for the pupil, and an English - Malayalam Dictionary, to the availability of an environment for learning. The subject is required to respond to each item by marking their availability at home (using 'yes' or 'No'). Each 'Yes' response receive a 'unit' score while 'No' response receive a zero score . The score of a subject is the sum of the scores obtained by him in all the eighteen items of the inventory.

The authors of the inventory report that the items have been selected by six judges who are specialists in different social sciences – sociology, education and psychology.

Validity and Reliability

The validity of the inventory has been assured in terms of the definition and representation given to the concept under measurement (construct and concurrent validity). A crude form external validation is also reported. The scores of the inventory was correlated with total class achievement of 85 pupils of standard. IX in a selected secondary school. A correlation of 0.41 is reported by the authors of the test.

The split - half reliability coefficient of the test (worked out using the sample used for the external validation study reported above) as reported by the authors is 0.69. The test on the whole is a reasonably valid and reliable instrument for measuring, the construct of 'home learning facility' under Kerala conditions.

(xiii) General Achievement Test for Standard IX

The investigator developed and standardised achievement test in six academic subjects, namely Malayalam, English, Hindi, General Science, Social Studies and Mathematics included in the curriculum for Standard IX. Since the test preparation demanded vast experience in the field, the help of experts and experienced teachers was sought. A number of teachers and specialists in educational evaluation were contacted by the investigator. With their support and help she was able to prepare multiple choice items in the subject areas. Each item was framed with four multiple choice answers. Care was taken to ensure that all areas for Standard IX were fully represented. The specialists were experienced teachers with adequate familiarity with construction of objective type items.

The test items prepared by the teachers and by the investigator herself were edited and arranged with the help of specialists in the Department of Education. The items were checked against a blue print prepared by the investigator for this purpose. It was decided that each subject test should include 25 test items in the final form, and hence 50 items were included in each subject before standardisation. This was to provide a wider choice for the selection of the final items. The final scrutiny and arrangement of the items were done by the investigator with the help of supervising teacher and two subject members for each subject. The items were selected and arranged by observing carefully all the rules set for preparing objective type questions. The arrangements of distracters were arranged in such a way that the position of the correct choice would occur in a random order through out the test.

The items finally selected were compiled into a test form. The items were arranged in the increasing order of difficulty as decided by experts. Separate answer sheet was prepared and supplied for marking the answers. The students were given instruction as how to mark the answer of an item on the multiple response answer-sheet.

The try-out of the test for item analysis was conducted on a sample of 170 pupils attending Standard IX. The response sheets of the 170 pupils were used for item analysis. The process of item analysis helped to identify items with high discriminating power and optimum difficulty level. Items were scored by assigning one score for each correct response and zero score for a wrong answer. The responses of the top scoring 27 per cent of the response sheets and the bottom scoring 27 per cent were used for item analysis.

In selecting items, the highest discriminating power was combined with optimum difficulty index. The best 25 items from each sub-test came to be selected. The selected items were arranged in the order of difficulty, with simplest items giving at the beginning and more difficult items appearing towards at the end of the test. Separate time limit was allocated for each sub-test after observing the time taken by pupils to finish different subjects.

The details of the content of the final test is presented in Table 8.

TABLE 8 : DETAILS OF THE SUB – TESTS IN THE ACHIEVEMENT TEST FOR STANDARD IX.

	Sub-test	Number of Items	Time in Minutes
1.	Malayalam	23	8
2.	English	25	12
3.	Hindi	25	10
4.	Social Studies	24	10
5.	General Science	25	10
6.	Mathematics	25	12

The format of the final test and score sheet were exactly the same as the one used for the draft test.

Validity and Reliability

The validity and reliability of the achievement test was assessed before it was used in the final data collection. The validity of each of the sub-test was compared with the average of the pupils' three preceding class examination marks expressed as percentages. The sub-test in Malayalam was compared with class examination marks in Malayalam, and similarly for other subjects. A sample of 85 pupils studying in two class divisions in Standard IX was used for the purpose. The sample consisted of 40 boys and 45 girls. The correlation coefficients (validity) are given in Table 9.

TABLE 9 VALIDITY COEFFICIENTS OF GENERAL ACHIEVEMENT TEST FOR STANDARD IX.

Subject	Correlation coefficient (r) with class examination marks
Malayalam	0.54
English	0.49
Hindi	0.58
Social Studies	0.47
General Science	0.49
Mathematics	0.52

The reliability of the sub-tests was estimated using the split-half procedure. Here the odd numbered items are treated as one half of the test and scored separately and all the even numbered items are treated as another half and scored. The scores of the two tests are correlated. The coefficient of correlations (reliability) are given in Table 10.

TABLE 10: RELIABILITY COEFFICIENTS OF GENERAL ACHIEVEMENT TEST FOR STANDARD IX.

Subject	Split-half reliability
Malayalam	0.84
English	0.79
Hindi	0.78
Social Studies	0.72
General Science	0.85
Mathematics	0.76

The calculated coefficients are adequately high to warrant the acceptable levels of validity and reliability of the test.

(xiv) The Kerala Socio - economic Scale

This tool developed by Nair (1976) is a popular research tool which measures Socio-economic Status. It measures the individual's Father's education level, Father's occupation level and Father's income level. An equal weightage is given for Mother's education level, Mother's occupation level and Mother's income level.

The income levels were slightly modified, with respect to the responses collected, according to the latest income ratings. The tool is in the form of a questionnaire, which in addition to obtaining data for quantifying socio-economic status, is also of help in obtaining personal information relating to each subject.

Parent's education level, Parent's occupation level, Parent's income level and hence the socio-economic status have been determined by quantifying the data, giving weightages as described in Table 11.

TABLE 11 : SCORING SCHEME OF THE KERALA SOCIO ECONOMIC SCALE

Variables		Categories	Weightage
Parent's Education Level	1	M.A./ M.Sc/ M.Com / M.B.B.S. / M.Ed. / B.Sc. (Engg.) L.L.B, etc.	10
	2	B.A. / B.Sc./ B.Com. / Diploma in Engg., etc.	8
	3	Pre-University/Pre-Degree/ T.T.C/ I.T.I.;etc.	5
	4	Standard VIII to X	3
	5	Standard I to VII	2
	6	Illiterate	0
Parent's Occupation Level	1	High professional	10
	2	Semi – Professional	9
	3	Skilled	8
	4	Semi-skilled	5
	5	Unskilled	3
	6	Unemployed	0
Parent's Income Level	1	Above Rs.5000/-	5
	2	Rs.3001/- to Rs.5000/-	4
	3	Rs.1501/- to Rs.3000/-	3
	4	Rs.501/- to Rs.1500/-	2
	5	Up to Rs.500/-	1

The procedure of quantifying 'Father's Occupation Level' is given below. This has been classified into six categories. These are as follows :

High professionals

Ministers, judges, bank executives and officials, doctors, engineers, lawyers, university teachers, heads of research organisations, heads of government departments, secretaries of government, big landlords, business executives, etc., belong to this category and a 10 point score is allotted to this category.

Semi-professionals

Chemists, druggists, qualified nurses, managers, superintendents of offices, minor businessmen, contractors, small landlords, sub inspectors of police, sub-registrars, assistant educational officers, block development officers, officers of sub district level, public health workers, etc., come under this category and they are assigned a 9 point score.

Skilled

Mechanics, fitters, electricians, drivers, photographers, laboratory assistants, carpenters, document workers, vakil clerks, head constables, village officers etc., fall under this category and they are assigned a 8 point score.

Semi-skilled

Farmers, small-scale merchants, library attenders, police constables, etc. belong to this category and they are assigned a 5 point score.

Unskilled

Coolies, ordinary labourers, watchmen, peons, etc., form the unskilled groups. A 3 point score is assigned to this group.

Unemployed

Those who have no work at all. No weightage is assigned to this category (zero score).

Summated score for 'Parent's Education Level', 'Parent's Occupation Level' and 'Parent's Income Level' (with equal weightage given for both) is taken as the score for 'Family Education Level' of an individual.

Sample used for the study

The sample for the study was selected in such a way as to yield generalisable results from the study. This required certain basic decisions to be taken regarding the sample. Decision had to be taken relating to the following aspects :

a. Size of the sample.

b. Techniques of sampling

c. Factors to be represented in the sample.

(a) Size of the sample

The size of the sample should be adequate for statistical analyses to be employed, hence making the interpretation of the collected data, easy and effective. Guilford (1954) in his 'Psychometric Method', gives guidelines regarding sample size. According to him, when Pearson's r is used, a minimum number of 200 is a good policy. Garrett (1966) also ,mostly confirms this view and states that the larger the sample size (N), the larger the standard deviation (s) of the sample and the more inclusive (and presumably representative) the sample becomes, of the general population. He has also shown that a sample of 200 (N = 200) drawn from a normal population covers the range from $\pm$ 3 s where s is the standard deviation of the distribution. Thus, a sample size of 200 can yield reliable results for a study. The size should be small enough to permit a close study since there are a series of other tests to be administered in each group. It was estimated that 4 to 6 hours of testing time will have to be utilized for each group. The above considerations, together with the need to use stratified random sampling suggested a sample of around 1000.

(b) Techniques of sampling

Of the various techniques of sampling used in social science researches, the investigator decided to adopt the technique of 'stratified random sampling' for the purpose of the present study. This technique is applicable when the population is composed of subgroups or strata of different sizes so that a representative sample must contain individuals drawn from each category or stratum in accordance with the size of the subgroups.

(c) Factors to be represented in the sample

The next major decision to be taken regarding sampling was the factors to be represented in the sample selection. Due representation is to be given to the basic factors which would possibly be influence the performance of pupils. As such, it was decided to give representation to the following factors in the sample selection:

(i) Rural – urban residence of subjects

(ii) Sex of subjects

(iii) Institutional type, viz., Government-Private schools.

The study was confined to the southern part of Kerala for easy access; and 25 schools were selected. These schools contain all categories of students and is fairly representative of the students of Kerala State. Then it was decided to give due representation to the locale (Rural : Urban = 2:1), sex of subjects (Boy : Girl=1: 2) and institutional type (Government: Private = 1:1). On the basis of the above consideration an initial break up of a tentative sample was worked out. On the assumption that a final sample of 900 will be available for analysis, it was decided to cover a larger basal sample of 1200. For 1200 subjects, the numbers to be covered for each stratum was estimated. The details are presented in Table 12.

TABLE 12 BREAK - UP OF THE BASAL SAMPLE IN TERMS OF SEX AND RESIDENCE

	Boys	Girls	Total
Urban	175	275	450
Rural	250	500	750
Total	425	775	1200

The number of class divisions to be tested for each category was worked out assuming that the minimum strength of the class will not be less than 30.

Three types of schools are in existence in the State of Kerala, viz., Boy's schools, Girl's schools and Mixed schools. The divisions were so chosen as to give adequate representation to the two sexes. A list of schools to be covered was prepared, considering all the variables to be represented, etc.

The final sample available for analysis

The total sample tested was 996. The whole sample was not usable because some of the pupils had not completed all the tests. In most of the schools, the testing had to be conducted on two different occasions. So when a pupil was absent for any one test session, the remaining data was not usable. Rejecting all such cases, a final sample of 879 was available for analysis. The details of the final sample are given in Tables 13 and 14.

TABLE 13: BREAK-UP OF THE ACTUAL SAMPLE COVERED

	Boys	Girls	Total
Urban	148	196	344
Rural	239	413	652
Total	387	609	996

TABLE 14 : BREAK - UP OF THE FINAL SAMPLE USED FOR ANALYSIS

	Boys	Girls	Total
Urban	103	172	275
Rural	206	398	604
Total	309	570	879

Data Collection Procedures

After finalising the sample and tools to be used, a programme for testing was arranged after visiting the selected schools. The investigator met the heads of the schools and the class teachers and had discussions with them; their co -operation was thus assured. The investigator studied the basic literature relating to the selected psychological tests contained in the test manuals and other references and acquainted herself with the testing procedures, possible eventualities, etc., before commencing actual testing. She then obtained copies of the test booklets and the answer sheets in the final form in adequate numbers.

All the tests were administered with the help of classroom teachers. An interval of 5-15 minutes was allowed in between two tests.

The test batteries were administered in selected schools in two sittings of about three-hour sessions each day. The investigator got the help of the class teachers in administering the tests. The investigator gave a short explanation of the aim and scope of the study to the subjects and appealed to their conscious participation and co-operation. The tasks implied in answering each test was explained before each test was given. An interval of 5 to 15 minutes was allowed in between two tests. The rules and procedures prescribed for each test in the manuals were strictly followed. Uniform procedures were observed in administering the tests in the different schools.

The following steps were invariably followed for administering the tests :

(i) Distribution of the test booklets to the subjects together with printed instructions regarding the test.

(ii) Explaining the general directions in the booklet.

(iii) Distribution of answer sheets with instructions for filling them up.

(iv) Making the students familiar with the answer sheets, method of entering responses, etc.

(v) Clearing the doubts of subjects, giving instructions regarding time-limit, methods of dealing with eventualities, etc.

(vi) Strict adherence to the time-limit in the case of speed tests, directions not to disfigure the booklets, etc.

(vii) Giving intervals between testing.

(viii) Collecting back the test booklets and answer sheets.

Scoring and Consolidation of Data

The response sheets of all the tests were scored as per the scoring scheme of the tests, described earlier along with each test. All the relevant data relating to each subject, test scores in the case of different variables, and the demographic details like age, sex, name of school, class with division, place of residence, whether rural or urban, type of school, etc., were entered separately on specifically designed sheets of paper. The data was either in the numerical form or in the descriptive form which again was indicated by number codes. Only those subjects for whom complete data was available were retained for analysis. The data (consolidated following a standard pattern with a code number assigned for each test. etc.) were entered in a form appropriate for computer data processing.

Processing of data

Most of the computations were done by computers. The calculations relating to the identification of discrepant achievers in each of the six school subjects were computed by hand. The different computations and their interpretations extended for a few months.

Identification of Discrepant Achievers

The details of the procedures adopted in identifying underachievers and overachievers (discrepant achievers) in all the six school subjects separately from among a sample of 879 on the basis of scores assigned to each subject in intelligence and school subjects Malayalam, English, Hindi, Social Studies, General Science and Mathematics are given below:

IDENTIFICATION OF DISCREPANT ACHIEVERS IN RESPECT OF EACH OF THE SIX SCHOOL SUBJECTS

Identification of Discrepant Achievers (viz., underachievers and overachievers) in six school subjects from a total sample of 879 subjects was done on the basis of scores assigned to each pupil in six school subjects, viz., Malayalam, English, Hindi, Social Studies, Science, Mathematics and Intelligence: Total. The details of the procedures are given below:

(i) Identification of underachievers and over achievers in Malayalam

Correlation between Malayalam achievement and Intelligence: Total (Verbal and non-verbal) was calculated. Mean and standard deviation of scores on Malayalam achievement and Intelligence were also calculated. A Regression Equation (Garrett , 1966) between Intelligence and Malayalam achievement was worked out. The details of the calculations used for developing the regression equation are given below:

Intelligence (X)	Malayalam Achievement (Y)
$M_x = 85.24$	$M_y = 12.18$
$\sigma_x = 28.11$	$\sigma_y = 4.74$

$$r_{xy} = 0.5721$$

Where M_x = Mean of Intelligence : Total

M_y = Mean of Malayalam Achievement

σ_x = Standard deviation of Intelligence: Total

σ_y = Standard deviation of Malayalam Achievement

r_{xy} = Correlation between Intelligence: Total and Malayalam Achievement. score

Standard score form of the regression equation is

$$\bar{Y} = r_{xy} \frac{\sigma_y}{\sigma_x} X$$

In raw scores

$$Y - M_y = r_{xy} \frac{\sigma_y}{\sigma_x} (X - M_x)$$

$$\text{ie. } Y = r_{xy} \frac{\sigma_y}{\sigma_x} (X - M_x) + M_y$$

$$Y = 0.5721 \times \frac{4.74}{28.11} (X - 85.24) + 12.18$$

$$Y = 0.096\, X + 3.96$$

Most probable X = 85.24

Substituting 85.24 for X in the above equation, the most probable

$$Y = 0.096 \times 85.24 + 3.96 = 12.18$$

The standard error of Y (predicated from an X score) was calculated using the formula

$$\sigma_{est.y} = y\sqrt{1 - r^2}$$

$$= 4.74 \sqrt{1 - (0.5721)^2}$$

$$= 3.8876$$

Under achievers in Malayalam were then identified by the method used by Farquhar (1963). For classifying the subjects into three levels (underachievers, normal achievers and overachievers), the regression equation Y = 0.096 X + was plotted on a graph paper. Two lines parallel with this line and at a vertical distance of 3.887 units (s est.y) were marked both above and below the line (Figure 1). The portion contained between these lines (dotted in the figure) was marked as the region containing normal achievers. The zone

FIGURE 1 : REGRESSION EQUATION AND LIMITS USED FOR IDENTIFYING DISCREPANT ACHIEVERS IN MALAYALAM

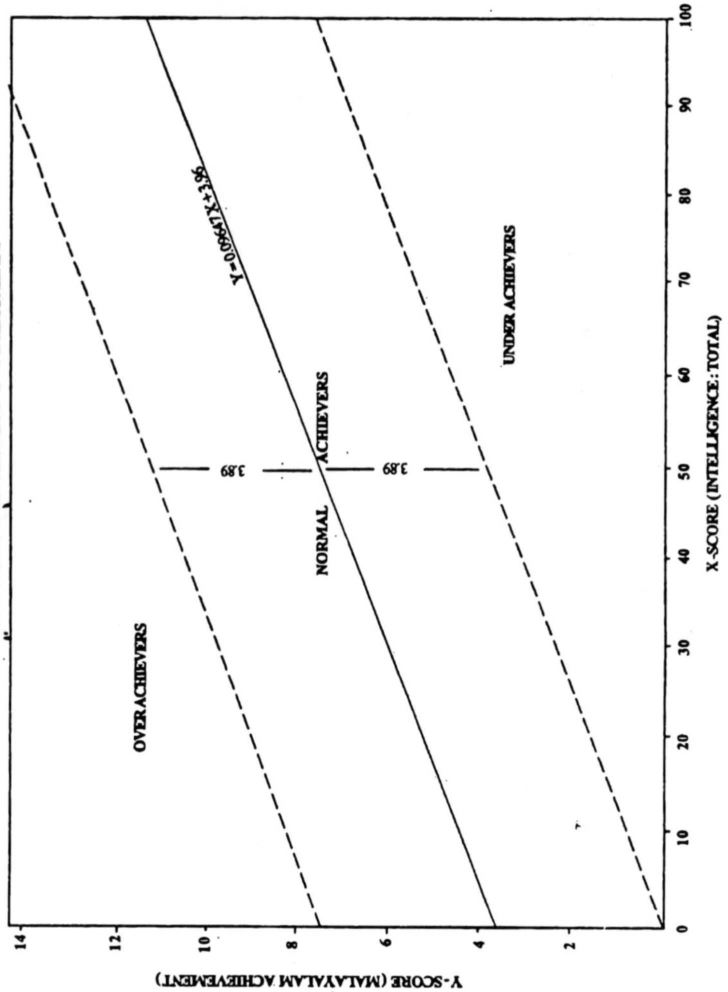

below was marked as the region for the underachievers and the region above the zone was marked as the region for overachievers. With the help of this figure a subject was classified as follows:

Let X_r represent the subject's Intelligence score and Y_r denote his Malayalam achievement score. The subject could be represented as a point (X_r, Y_r) using two dimensional Cartesian Co-ordinate system. In the figure given (Figure 1), if the point (X_r, Y_r) falls in the middle domain of the first quadrant (dotted space) he is regarded as a normal achiever. If the point falls into the domain above the dotted portion in the first quadrant, then the individual is classified as an overachiever, and if the individual falls in the portion below the dotted area, in the same quadrant, the individual is classified as an underachiever.

All the 879 subjects were classified by this method. The classification yielded 114 underachievers, 653 normal achievers and 112 overachievers. The break-up of the underachievers and overachievers in Malayalam is presented in Table 15

TABLE 15 : BREAK-UP OF THE DISCREPANT ACHIEVERS AND NON DISCREPANT ACHIEVERS IN MALAYALAM

	Discrepant Achievers			Non Discrepant Achievers	Total
	UA	OA	Total		
Boys	44	31	75	234	309
Girls	70	81	151	419	570
Total	114	112	226	653	879

UA - Under Achievers; OA - Over Achievers

(i) Identification of underachievers and overachievers in English

Correlation between Intelligence: Total and English achievement was calculated. This was used to work out a regression equation between Intelligence: Total and English achievement. The details of the calculations used for developing the regression equation are presented below:

Intelligence (X)			English Achiev	
Mean (M_x)	=	85.24	Mean (M_y)	=
S.D. (σ_x	=	28.11	S.D. (σ_y)	=
r_{xy}	=	0.5589		

Standard score form of the regression equation in raw scores

$$\overline{Y} = 0.5589 \quad x \frac{4.94}{28.11}(X - 85.24) + 9.($$

$$\therefore Y = 0.09822\,X + 0.6377$$

$$\sigma_{est \cdot y} = 4.94\sqrt{1 - (0.5589)^2}$$

$$= 4.09$$

The regression equation Y=0.09822 x +0.6377 was plotted on a graph paper. Two lines parallel with this line and at a vertical distance of 4.09 units were marked both above and below the line (Figure 2). The zones for underachievers, normal achievers and overachievers were identified. The 879 subjects were classified into three groups by method described earlier. This classification yielded 406 underachievers, 431 normal achievers and 42 overachievers. The break-up of the underachievers and overachievers is given in Table 16.

FIGURE 2 : REGRESSION EQUATION AND LIMITS USED FOR IDENTIFYING DISCREPANT ACHIEVERS IN ENGLISH

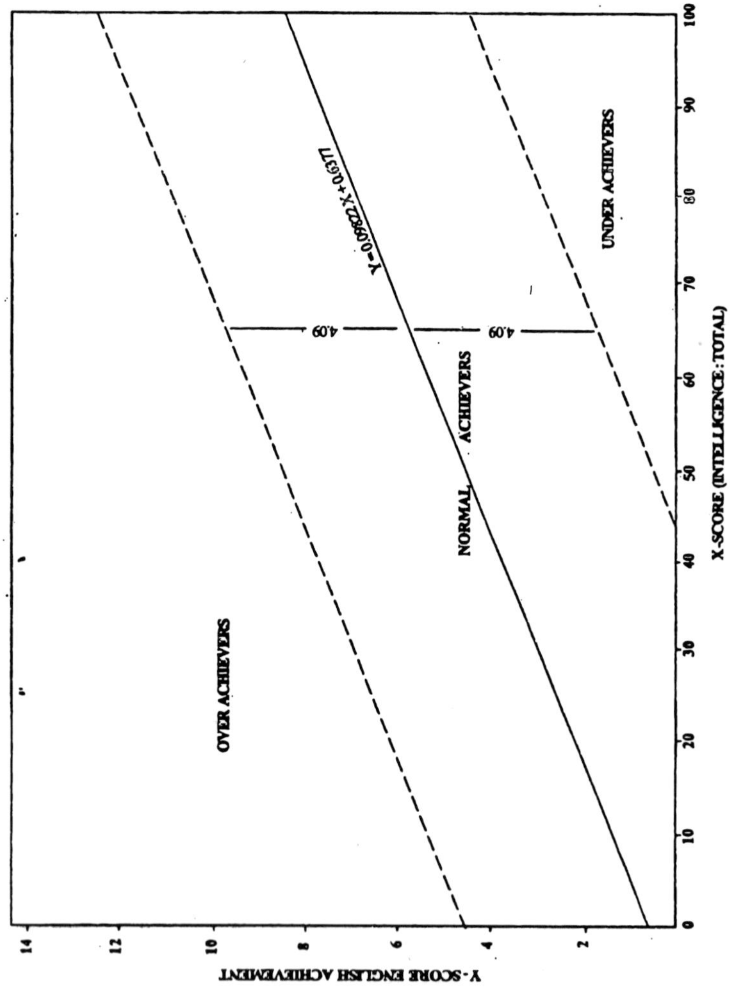

TABLE 16 BREAK - UP OF DISCREPANT ACHIEVERS AND NON -DISCREPANT ACHIEVERS IN ENGLISH

	Discrepant Achievers			Non Discrepant Achievers	Total
	UA	OA	Total		
Boys	184	16	200	109	309
Girls	222	26	248	322	570
Total	406	42	448	431	879

UA - Under Achievers; OA - Over Achievers

(i) Identification of underachievers and overachievers in Hindi

Correlation between Intelligence: Total and Hindi achievement was calculated. This was used to work out a regression equation between Intelligence: Total and Hindi achievement. The details of the calculations used for developing the regression equation are presented below :

Intelligence (X)		Hindi Achievement (Y)	
Mean (M_x)	= 85.24	Mean (M_y)	= 11.52
S.D. (σ_x)	= 28.11	S.D. (σ_y)	= 5.5524

$$r_{xy} = 0.6335$$

Standard score form of the regression equation in raw score is :

$$\overline{Y} = 0.6335 \ \text{x} \ \frac{5.5524}{28.11}(X - 85.24) + 11.52$$

$$\therefore Y = 0.1251 \ X + 0.853$$

$$\sigma_{est.y} = 5.5524 \ \text{x} \ \sqrt{1 - 0.6335^2}$$

$$= 4.296$$

FIGURE 3 : REGRESSION EQUATION AND LIMITS USED FOR IDENTIFYING DISCREPANT ACHIEVERS IN HINDI

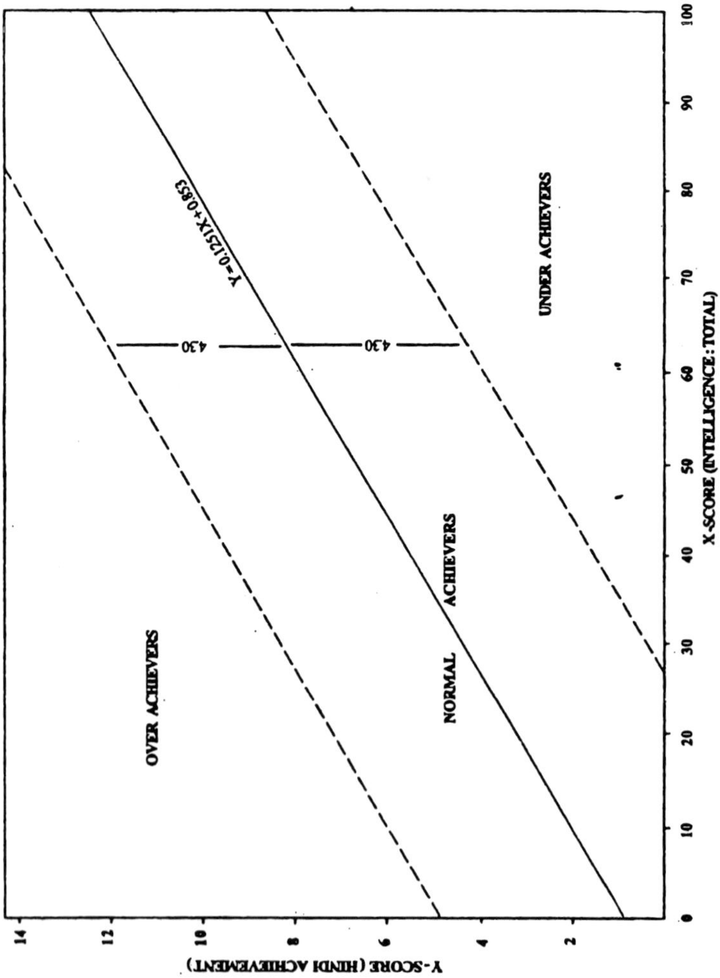

The regression equation Y=0.1251 x +0.853 was plotted on a graph paper. Two lines parallel with this line and at a vertical distance of 4.30 units were marked both above and below the line (Figure 3). The 879 subjects were classified into three groups by method described earlier. This classification yielded 137 underachievers 621 normal achievers and 121 overachievers. The break-up of the underachievers and overachievers is given in Table 17.

TABLE 17 : BREAK-UP OF DISCREPANT ACHIEVERS AND NON DISCREPANT ACHIEVERS IN HINDI

	Discrepant Achievers			Non Discrepant Achievers	Total
	UA	OA	Total		
Boys	54	41	95	214	309
Girls	83	80	163	407	570
Total	137	121	258	621	879

UA - Under Achievers ; OA - Over Achievers

(i) Identification of underachievers and overachievers in Social Studies

Correlation between Intelligence: Total and Social Studies achievement was calculated. This was used to workout a regression equation between Intelligence: Total and Social Studies achievement. The details of the calculations used for developing the regression equation are presented below:

Mean (M_x) = 85.24 Mean (M_y) = 10.24

S.D. (σ_x) = 28.11 S.D. (σ_y) = 5.02

$r_{xy} = 0.5924$

$$\overline{Y} = 0.5924 \times \frac{5.02}{28.1099}(X - 8524) + 10.24$$

$$\therefore \overline{Y} = 0.1058\,X + 1.22$$

$$\sigma_{est.y} = 5.02 \times \sqrt{1 - 0.5924^2}$$
$$= 4.04$$

The regression equation Y=0.1058 x +1.22 was plotted on a graph paper. Two lines parallel with this line and at a vertical distance of 4.04 units were marked both above and below the line (Figure 4). The 879 subjects were classified into three groups by method described earlier. This classification yielded 119 underachievers, 636 normal achievers and 124 overachievers. The break-up of the underachievers and overachievers is given in Table 18.

TABLE 18 BREAK-UP OF DISCREPANT ACHIEVERS AND NON DISCREPANT ACHIEVERS IN SOCIAL STUDIES

	Discrepant Achievers			Non Discrepant Achievers	Total
	UA	OA	Total		
Boys	47	26	73	236	309
Girls	72	98	170	400	570
Total	119	124	243	636	879

UA - Under Achievers; OA - Over Achievers

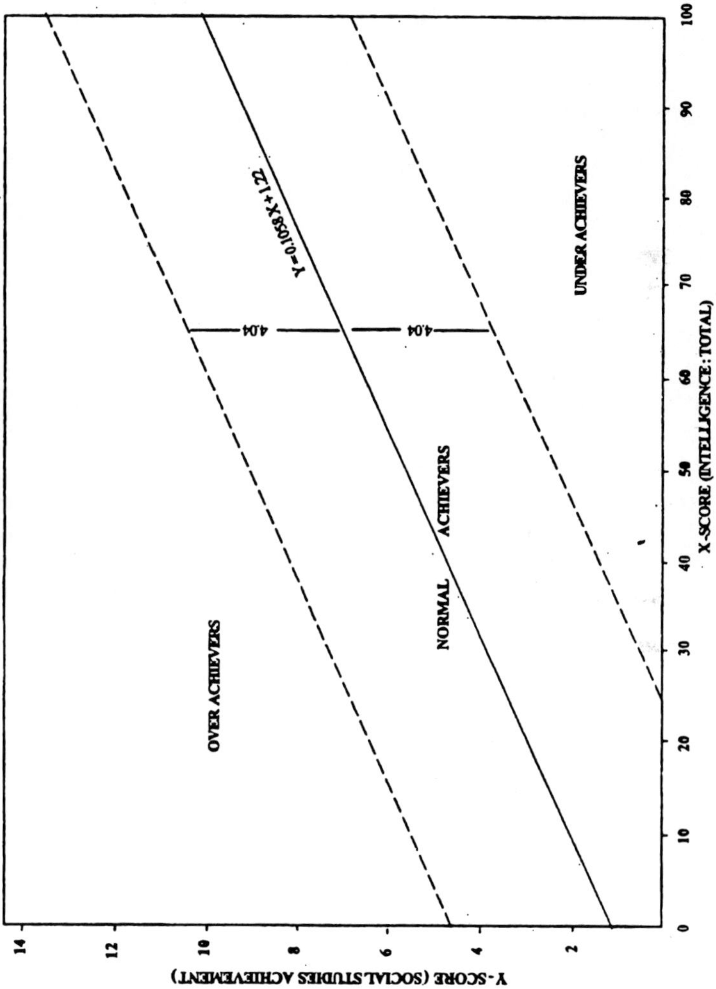

FIGURE 4 : REGRESSION EQUATION AND LIMITS USED FOR IDENTIFYING DISCREPANT ACHIEVERS IN SOCIAL STUDIES

(i) Identification of underachievers and overachievers in Science

Correlation between Intelligence: Total and Science achievement was calculated. This was used to work out a regression equation between Intelligence: Total and Science achievement. The details of the calculations used for developing the regression equation are presented below:

Intelligence (X)		Science Achievement (Y)	
Mean (M_x) =	85.24	Mean (My) =	11.32
S.D (σx) =	28.11	S.D. (σy) =	5.269

$$r_{xy} = 0.5399$$

$$\overline{Y} = 0.6335 \times \frac{5.5524}{28.11}(X - 85.24) + 11.52$$

$$\therefore \overline{Y} = 0.1012X + 2.69$$

$$\sigma_{est.y} = 5.269 \times \sqrt{1 - 0.5399^2}$$

$$= 4.43$$

The regression equation Y=0.1012 x +2.69 was plotted on a graph paper. Two lines parallel with this line and at a vertical distance of 4.43 units were marked both above and below the line (Figure 5). The 879 subjects were classified into three groups by method described earlier. This classification yielded 118 underachievers, 635 normal achievers and 126 overachievers. The break-up of the underachievers and overachievers is given in Table 19.

TABLE 19. BREAK-UP OF DISCREPANT ACHIEVERS AND NON DISCREPANT ACHIEVERS IN SCIENCE

	Discrepant Achievers			Non Discrepant Achievers	Total
	UA	OA	Total		
Boys	45	40	85	224	309
Girls	73	86	159	411	570
Total	118	126	244	635	879

U A - Under Achievers OA - Over Achievers

FIGURE 5 : REGRESSION EQUATION AND LIMITS USED FOR IDENTIFYING DISCREPANT ACHIEVERS IN SCIENCE

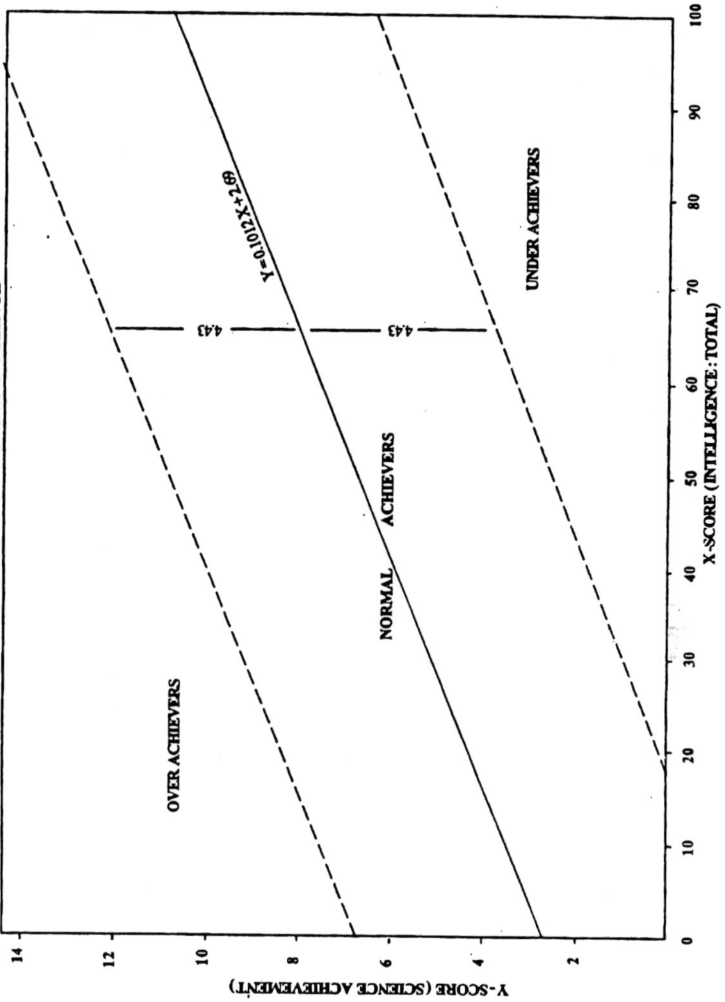

(vi) Identification of underachievers and overachievers in Mathematics

Correlation between Intelligence: Total and Mathematics achievement was calculated. This was used to work out a regression equation between Intelligence: Total and Mathematics achievement. The details of the calculations used for developing the regression equation are presented below:

Intelligence (X)		Mathematics Achievement (Y)	
Mean (M_x) =	85.24	Mean (My) =	8.25
S.D. (sx) =	28.11	S.D. (sy) =	4.63

$r_{xy} = 0.4750$

$$\overline{Y} = 0.4750 \times \frac{4.63}{28.1099}(X - 85.24) + 8.25$$

$$\overline{Y} = 0..07824\ X + 1.581$$

$$\sigma_{est.\,y} = 4.63 \times \sqrt{1 - 0.4750^2}$$

$$= 4.074$$

The regression equation Y=0.7824 x +1.581 was plotted on a graph paper. Two lines parallel with this line and at a vertical distance of 4.07 units were marked both above and below the line (Figure 6). The 879 subjects were classified into three groups by method described earlier. This classification yielded 125 underachievers, 661 normal achievers and 93 overachievers. The break-up of the underachievers and overachievers is given in Table 20.

TABLE 20 BREAK-UP OF DISCREPANT ACHIEVERS AND NON DISCREPANT ACHIEVERS IN MATHEMATICS

	Discrepant Achievers			Non Discrepant Achievers	Total
	UA	OA	Total		
Boys	58	21	79	230	309
Girls	67	72	139	431	570
Total	125	93	218	661	879

UA – Under Achiever ; OA – Over Achievers

FIGURE 6 : REGRESSION EQUATION AND LIMITS USED FOR IDENTIFYING DISCREPANT ACHIEVERS IN MATHEMATICS

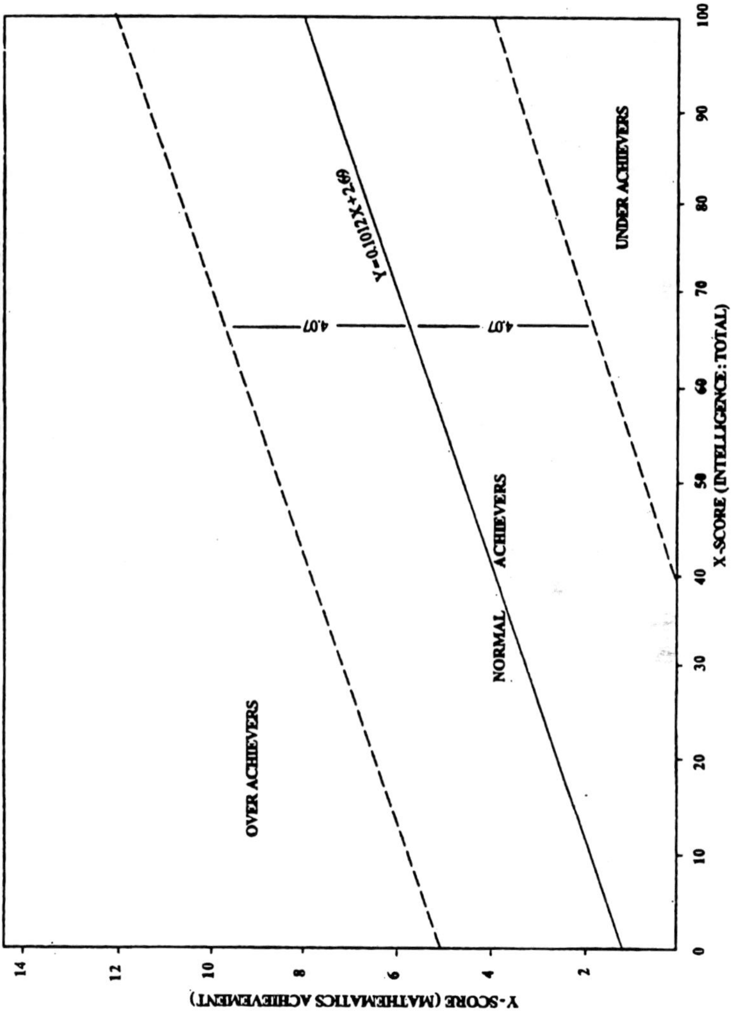

Processing of data

Consolidation of data sheets were prepared separately for the groups Discrepant Achievers (Over Achievers and Under Achievers) and Non Discrepant Achievers in each of the six school subjects. The data were entered in such a way that they could be used for computer data processing. The data were analysed and t - values were calculated.

Statistical Technique used in Analysing the data

Statistical analysis of the data were undertaken using procedures appropriate for the purpose of the study. The study used two-tailed test of significance of the difference between means for large independent groups. The ability of certain Psychological and Familial variables of discriminate between the different contrasted pairs of Discrepant Achievers and Non Discrepant Achievers in six school subjects was determined by testing the significance of the difference between means of the extreme pairs.

The procedure is to work out the t-value (called the critical ratio) given by the formula

$$t = \frac{M_1 - M_2}{SE_{M_1 - M_2}}$$

where M_1 = Mean test score for the first group

M_2 = Mean test score for the second group

SE_{M1-M2} = The standard error of the difference between means M_1 and M_2

SE_{M1-M2} is calculated by the formula

$$SE_{M1-M2} = \sqrt{SE_{M_1}^2 + SE_{M_2}^2}$$

Where SE_{M1} and SE_{M2} are the standard errors of the mean scores M_1 and M_2 respectively

If N_1 and N_2 are the size of the samples under comparison and σ_1 and σ_2 their standard deviations

Then

$$SE_{M_1} = \frac{\sigma_1}{\sqrt{N_1}}$$

$$SE_{M_2} = \frac{\sigma_1}{\sqrt{N_2}}$$

The obtained t - value (critical ratio) is then treated as belonging to a normal distribution. If the obtained t - value falls between -1.96 and +1.96 the difference between mean is said to be not significant at 0.05 level. In this case the difference is treated as the same as a zero difference. If the t - value falls outside the interval $\pm$ 1.96, then the difference is treated as significant at 0.05 level. This means that the difference is real and is greater than zero.

If the obtained t - value falls outside the interval $\pm$ 2.58, the difference is said to be significant at 0.01 level; otherwise the difference is not significant at 0.01 level. A significant difference between means imply that the difference is real and is different from zero.

CHAPTER 5

Analysis and Discussions

The major focus of the present investigation is the identification of a group of Psychological and Familial variables which can be used for discriminating between Discrepant Achievers (DA : 1.Under Achievers 2. Over Achievers) and Non Discrepant Achievers (NDA) in various school subjects. Any significant difference indicated in a pair under comparison is interpreted as showing the ability of the concerned variable to discriminate between the pairs. The pairs compared in this section of the analysis are indicated below :

i. DA (UA) and NDA (Malayalam)

ii. DA (OA) and NDA (Malayalam)

iii. DA (UA) and NDA (English)

iv. DA (OA) and NDA (English)

v. DA (UA) and NDA (Hindi)

vi. DA (OA) and NDA (Hindi)

vii. DA (UA) and NDA (Social Studies)

viii. DA (OA) and NDA (Social Studies)

ix. DA (UA) and NDA Science)

x DA (OA) and NDA (Science)

xi. DA (UA) and NDA (Mathematics)

xii. DA (OA) and NDA Mathematics)

1. Comparison of Discrepant Achievers (Under Achievers) and Non Discrepant Achievers in Malayalam with respect to each of the Psychological and Familial variables.

Means of Psychological and Familial variables of Discrepant Achievers (Under Achievers) and Non Discrepant Achievers were compared using two - tailed tests of significance. Information regarding the results of tests of significance for the different Psychological and Familial variables of Discrepant Achievers (Under Achievers) and Non Discrepant Achievers in Malayalam are given in Table 21.

TABLE 21 : STATISTICAL DATA AND RESULTS OF THE TESTS OF SIGNIFICANCE FOR DIFFERENCE BETWEEN MEANS OF THE PSYCHOLOGICAL AND FAMILIAL VARIABLES OF DISCREPANT ACHIEVERS (UNDERACHIEVERS) AND NON DISCREPANT ACHIEVERS IN MALAYALAM.

	Variables	DA (UA)		NDA		Critical Ratio
		Mean M_1	S.D σ_1	Mean M_2	S.D σ_2	
1.	Personal Adjustment	50.16	8.99	52.62	10.28	2.64**
2.	Social Adjustment	47.00	10.97	49.98	10.78	2.68**
3.	General Anxiety	14.36	5.01	14.96	4.81	1.19
4.	Examination Anxiety	12.81	4.89	12.64	5.06	0.34
5.	Introversion-extraversion	11.65	3.22	12.11	3.51	1.39
6.	Masculinity- femininity	10.23	4.01	10.18	4.40	0.12
7.	Achievement Motivation	27.38	5.25	27.15	6.24	0.42
8.	Family Education Level	5.39	3.05	5.69	3.08	0.94
9.	Family Cultural Level	23.16	5.54	23.95	4.95	1.43
10.	Family Environment	16.61	4.53	16.79	4.46	0.39
11.	Family Acceptance	22.54	5.16	23.13	4.95	1.13
12.	Home Learning Facility	10.33	3.48	1.87	3.40	1.53
		N_1 = 114		N_2 = 653		

*Significant at 0.05 level ** Significant at 0.01 level

It is seen from Table 21 that Discrepant Achievers (Under Achievers) and Non Discrepant Achievers in Malayalam differ significantly at 0.01 level in Personal Adjustment variable and Social Adjustment variable. In both the variables, Non Discrepant Achievers scored higher means than that scored by Discrepant Achievers (Under Achievers).

The discriminating variables in the order of importance (in the descending order of the absolute value of critical ratio) are:

Social Adjustment (CR = 2.68)

Personal Adjustment (CR = 2.64)

In all the remaining variables (General Anxiety, Examination Anxiety, Introversion – extraversion, Masculinity – femininity, Family Environment, Family Acceptance and Home Learning Facility) the difference between Discrepant Achievers (Under Achievers) and Non Discrepant Achievers in Malayalam is not significant.

2. Comparison of Discrepant Achievers (Over Achievers) and Non Discrepant Achievers in Malayalam with respect to each of the Psychological and Familial variables

The statistical indices and the results of the tests of significance for the twelve Psychological and Familial variables for Discrepant Achievers (Over Achievers) and Non Discrepant Achievers in Malayalam are presented in Table 22.

The above table shows that out of the twelve variables used in this study, five variables are capable of discriminating between Discrepant Achievers (Over Achievers) and Non Discrepant Achievers in Malayalam.

The variables in the order of importance are :

Family Education Level (CR = 5.15)

Social Adjustment (CR = 3.26)

Home Learning Facility (CR = 2.93)

General Anxiety (CR = 2.44)

Achievement Motivation (CR = 2.04)

TABLE 22 : STATISTICAL DATA AND RESULTS OF TESTS OF SIGNIFICANCEFOR THE DIFFERENCE BETWEEN MEANS OF THE PSYCHOLOGICAL AND FAMILIAL VARIABLES OF DISCREPANT ACHIEVERS (OVER ACHIEVERS) AND NON DISCREPANT ACHIEVERS IN MALAYALAM.

Variables		DA (OA)		NDA		Critical Ratio
		Mean M_1	S.D σ_1	Mean M_2	S.D σ_2	
1.	Personal Adjustment	54.10	11.10	52.62	10.28	1.32
2.	Social Adjustment	53.81	11.62	49.98	10.78	3.26**
3.	General Anxiety	13.92	4.05	14.96	4.81	2.44*
4.	Examination Anxiety	12.54	3.60	12.11	3.51	0.95
5.	Introversion-extraversion	12.46	3.60	12.11	3.51	0.95
6.	Masculinity- femininity	9.40	4.68	10.18	4.40	1.64
7.	Achievement Motivation	28.47	6.35	27.15	6.24	2.04*
8.	Family Education Level	7.46	3.41	5.69	3.08	5.15**
9.	Family Cultural Level	24.82	4.42	23.95	4.93	1.89
10.	Family Environment	16.37	4.48	16.79	4.46	0.92
11.	Family Acceptance	23.20	4.76	23.13	4.95	0.14
12.	Home Learning Facility	11.90	3.45	10.87	3.40	2.93**
		$N_1 = 112$		$N_2 = 653$		

* Significant at 0.05 level ** Significant at 0.01 level

Discrepant Achievers (Over Achievers) secured higher mean scores than Non Discrepant Achievers in the variables Family Education Level, Social Adjustment, Home Learning Facility and Achievement Motivation. In General Anxiety the higher mean is found to be associated with Non Discrepant Achievers.

Of the five variables, Family Education Level, Social Adjustment and Home Learning Facility discriminate the Discrepant Achievers (Over Achievers) and Non Discrepant Achievers in Malayalam at 0.01 level. The variables, General Anxiety and Achievement Motivation discriminate the two groups at 0.05 level .

For the remaining variables (Personal Adjustment , Examination Anxiety, Introversion – extraversion, Masculinity – femininity, Family Cultural Level, Family Environment and Family Acceptance)the difference between Discrepant Achievers (Over Achievers) and Non Discrepant Achievers in Malayalam is not significant.

3. Comparison of Discrepant Achievers (Under Achievers) and Non Discrepant Achievers in English with respect to each of the Psychological and Familial variables

Means of Psychological and Familial variables of Discrepant Achievers (Under Achievers) and Non Discrepant Achievers were compared using two - tailed tests of significance. Information regarding the results of tests of significance for the different Psychological and Familial variables of Discrepant Achievers (Under Achievers) and Non Discrepant Achievers in English are given in Table 23.

The above table shows that out of the twelve variables used in this study only Family Education Level is capable of discriminating Discrepant Achievers (Under Achievers) and Non Discrepant Achievers in English at 0.01 level of significance. It can be seen that Non Discrepant Achievers have secured higher mean than Discrepant Achievers in the above variable.

TABLE 23 : STATISTICAL DATA AND RESULTS OF TESTS OF SIGNIFICANCE FOR DIFFERENCE BETWEEN MEANS OF THE PSYCHOLOGICAL AND FAMILIAL VARIABLES OF DISCREPANT ACHIEVERS (UNDER ACHIEVERS) AND NON DISCREPANT ACHIEVERS IN ENGLISH

	Variables	DA (UA)		NDA		Critical Ratio
		Mean M_1	S.D σ_1	Mean M_2	S.D σ_2	
1.	Personal Adjustment	51.83	9.81	52.39	9.84	0.82
2.	Social Adjustment	49.86	11.06	49.27	10.31	0.80
3.	General Anxiety	14.85	4.91	14.76	4.62	0.27
4.	Examination Anxiety	12.73	5.16	12.65	4.88	0.23
5.	Introversion-extraversion	11.78	3.33	12.24	3.61	1.92
6.	Masculinity- femininity	9.99	4.19	10.40	4.62	1.35
7.	Achievement Motivation	27.06	6.07	27.18	6.06	0.29
8.	Family Education Level	5.52	3.01	5.96	3.24	2.04*
9.	Family Cultural Level	23.81	5.24	24.06	4.78	0.72
10.	Family Environment	16.71	4.57	16.80	4.44	0.29
11.	Family Acceptance	22.98	5.12	23.20	4.86	0.64
12.	Home Learning Facility	10.73	3.35	11.01	3.54	1.18
		$N_1 = 406$		$N_2 = 431$		

* Significant at 0.05 level ** Significant at 0.01 level

In all the remaining variables (Personal Adjustment , Social Adjustment, General Anxiety, Examination Anxiety, Introversion – extraversion, Masculinity – femininity, Achievement Motivation, Family Cultural Level, Family Environment , Family Acceptance and Home Learning Facility) the difference between Discrepant Achievers (Under Achievers) and Non Discrepant Achievers in English is not significant.

4. Comparison of Discrepant Achievers (Over Achievers) and Non Discrepant Achievers in English with respect to each of the Psychological and Familial variables

The statistical indices and the results of the tests of significance for the twelve Psychological and Familial variables for Discrepant Achievers (Over Achievers) and Non Discrepant Achievers in English are presented in Table 24.

TABLE 24: STATISTICAL DATA AND RESULTS OF TESTS OF SIGNIFICANCE FOR DIFFERENCE BETWEEN MEANS OF THE PSYCHOLOGICAL AND FAMILIAL VARIABLES OF DISCREPANT ACHIEVERS (OVER ACHIEVERS) AND NON DISCREPANT ACHIEVERS IN ENGLISH.

	Variables	DA (OA)		NDA		Critical
		Mean	S.D	Mean	S.D	Ratio
		M_1	σ_1	M_2	σ_2	
1.	Personal Adjustment	59.90	15.19	52.39	9.84	3.14**
2.	Social Adjustment	60.50	12.98	49.27	10.31	5.44**
3.	General Anxiety	13.60	4.55	14.76	4.62	1.58
4.	Examination Anxiety	11.79	5.21	12.65	4.88	1.02
5.	Introversion-extraversion	13.76	3.18	12.24	3.61	2.92**
6.	Masculinity- femininity	7.90	3.08	10.40	4.62	4.76**
7.	Achievement Motivation	31.88	6.12	27.18	6.06	4.75**
8.	Family Education Level	8.38	3.19	5.96	3.24	4.69**
9.	Family Cultural Level	24.45	4.02	24.06	4.78	0.59
10.	Family Environment	15.81	3.65	16.80	4.44	1.64
11.	Family Acceptance	22.48	4.26	23.20	4.86	1.64
12.	Home Learning Facility	12.12	2.98	11.01	3.54	2.26*
		$N_1 = 42$		$N_2 = 431$		

* Significant at 0.05 level ** Significant at 0.01 level

The above table shows that out of the twelve variables used in this study, seven variables are capable of discriminating Discrepant Achievers (Over Achievers) and Non Discrepant Achievers in English.

The discriminating variables in the order of importance are :

Social Adjustment	(CR = 5.44)
Masculinity – femininity	(CR = 4.76)
Achievement Motivation	(CR = 4.75)
Family Education Level	(CR = 4.69)
Personal Adjustment	(CR = 3.14)
Introversion – extraversion	(CR = 2.92)
Home Learning Facility	(CR = 2.26)

Discrepant Achievers (Over Achievers) secured higher mean scores than Non Discrepant Achievers in all the variables discriminating Discrepant Achievers (Over Achievers) and Non Discrepant Achievers in English except in Masculinity - femininity. In Masculinity- femininity higher mean is found to be associated with Non Discrepant Achievers.

For the remaining variables, namely, General Anxiety , Examination Anxiety, Family Cultural Level, Family Environment and Family Acceptance the difference between Discrepant Achievers (Over Achievers) and Non Discrepant Achievers in English is not significant.

5. Comparison of Discrepant Achievers (Under Achievers) and Non Discrepant Achievers in Hindi with respect to each of the Psychological and Familial variables

Means of the Psychological and Familial variables of Discrepant Achievers (Under Achievers) and Non Discrepant Achievers were compared using two - tailed tests of significance. Information regarding the results of tests of significance for the different Psychological and Familial variables of Discrepant Achievers (Under Achievers) and Non Discrepant Achievers in Hindi are given in Table 25.

TABLE 25 : STATISTICAL DATA AND RESULTS OF TESTS OF SIGNIFICANCE FOR DIFFERENCE BETWEEN MEANS OF THE PSYCHOLOGICAL AND FAMILIAL VARIABLES OF DISCREPANT ACHIEVERS (UNDER ACHIEVERS) AND NON DISCREPANT ACHIEVERS IN HINDI

	Variables	DA (UA)		NDA		Critical Ratio
		Mean M_1	S.D σ_1	Mean M_2	S.D σ_2	
1.	Personal Adjustment	50.98	9.62	52.47	10.27	1.62
2.	Social Adjustment	48.34	11.3	49.81	10.74	1.39
3.	General Anxiety	15.11	4.60	14.67	4.85	1.00
4.	Examination Anxiety	13.74	5.56	12.47	5.04	2.46*
5.	Introversion-extraversion	11.93	3.22	11.98	3.53	0.16
6.	Masculinity- femininity	9.74	3.68	10.33	4.40	1.64
7.	Achievement Motivation	26.94	6.10	27.24	6.06	0.52
8.	Family Education Level	5.66	3.01	5.63	3.19	0.10
9.	Family Cultural Level	24.04	5.15	23.82	5.06	0.45
10.	Family Environment	16.85	4.36	16.73	4.56	0.29
11.	Family Acceptance	22.88	4.85	23.07	5.00	0.41
12.	Home Learning Facility	10.88	3.12	10.84	3.48	0.13
		$N_1 = 137$		$N_2 = 621$		

* Significant at 0.05 level ** Significant at 0.01 level

The above table shows that out of the twelve variables used in this study only Examination Anxiety variable (CR = 2.46) is capable of discriminating Discrepant Achievers (Under Achievers) and Non Discrepant Achievers in Hindi at 0.05 level of significance. It can be seen that higher mean in the above discriminating variable is associated with Discrepant Achievers.

In all the remaining variables (Personal Adjustment , Social Adjustment, General Anxiety, Introversion - Extraversion, Masculinity – femininity, Achievement Motivation, Family Education Level, Family Cultural Level, Family Environment , Family Acceptance and Home Learning Facility)the difference between Discrepant Achievers (Under Achievers) and Non Discrepant Achievers in Hindi is not significant.

6. **Comparison of Discrepant Achievers (Over Achievers) and Non Discrepant Achievers in Hindi with respect to each of the Psychological and Familial variables**

The statistical indices and the results of the tests of significance for the twelve Psychological and Familial variables for Discrepant Achievers (Over Achievers) and Non Discrepant Achievers in Hindi are presented in Table 26.

From Table 26 it can be seen that out of the twelve variables used in this study Social Adjustment, Introversion – extraversion and Family Education Level variables are capable of discriminating Discrepant Achievers (Over Achievers) and Non Discrepant Achievers in Hindi at 0.01 level of significance. Masculinity – femininity variable discriminates the two groups at 0.05 level of significance. Discrepant Achievers have secured higher mean score in all the discriminating variables than Non Discrepant Achievers.

The discriminating variables in the order of importance are :

Family Education Level (CR = 5.92)

Social Adjustment (CR = 3.19)

Introversion – extraversion (CR = 2.59)

Masculinity – femininity (CR =2.24)

In all the remaining variables (Personal Adjustment , General Anxiety, Examination Anxiety, Achievement Motivation, Family Cultural Level, Family Environment , Family Acceptance and Home Learning Facility) the difference between Discrepant Achievers

(Over Achievers) and Non Discrepant Achievers in Hindi is not significant.

TABLE 26 : STATISTICAL DATA AND RESULTS OF TESTS OF SIGNIFICANCE FOR DIFFERENCE BETWEEN MEANS OF THE PSYCHOLOGICAL AND FAMILIAL VARIABLES OF DISCREPANT ACHIEVERS (OVERACHIEVERS) AND NON DISCREPANT ACHIEVERS IN HINDI

	Variables	DA (OA)		NDA		Critical Ratio
		Mean M_1	S.D σ_1	Mean M_2	S.D σ_2	
1.	Personal Adjustment	54.27	10.76	52.47	10.27	1.70
2.	Social Adjustment	53.46	11.65	49.81	10.74	3.19**
3.	General Anxiety	14.71	4.44	14.67	4.85	0.09
4.	Examination Anxiety	12.33	4.16	12.47	5.04	0.33
5.	Introversion-extraversion	12.88	3.49	11.98	3.53	2.59**
6.	Masculinity- femininity	9.24	4.98	10.33	4.40	2.24*
7.	Achievement Motivation	28.37	6.57	27.24	6.06	1.75
8.	Family Education Level	7.39	2.95	5.63	3.19	5.92**
9.	Family Cultural Level	24.57	4.19	23.82	5.06	1.74
10.	Family Environment	16.48	4.14	16.73	4.56	0.60
11.	Family Acceptance	23.27	4.87	23.07	5.00	0.41
12.	Home Learning Facility	11.49	3.55	10.84	3.48	1.85
		$N_1 = 121$		$N_2 = 621$		

* Significant at 0.05 level ** Significant at 0.01 level

7. Comparison of Discrepant Achievers (Under Achievers) and Non Discrepant Achievers in Social Studies with respect to each of the Psychological and Familial variables

Means of the Psychological and Familial variables of Discrepant Achievers (Under Achievers) and Non Discrepant Achievers were compared using two - tailed tests of significance. Information regarding the results of tests of significance for the different Psychological and Familial variables of Discrepant Achievers (Under Achievers) and Non Discrepant Achievers in Social Studies are given in Table 27.

TABLE 27 : STATISTICAL DATA AND RESULTS OF TESTS OF SIGNIFICANCE FOR DIFFERENCE BETWEEN MEANS OF THE PSYCHOLOGICAL AND FAMILIAL VARIABLES DISCREPANT ACHIEVERS (UNDER ACHIEVERS) AND NON DISCREPANT ACHIEVERS IN SOCIAL STUDIES

	Variables	DA (UA)		NDA		Critical Ratio
		Mean M_1	S.D σ_1	Mean M_2	S.D σ_2	
1.	Personal Adjustment	51.16	9.42	52.36	10.36	1.25
2.	Social Adjustment	49.35	11.63	49.69	10.65	0.30
3.	General Anxiety	14.87	5.15	14.80	4.78	0.14
4.	Examination Anxiety	13.57	5.19	12.47	5.05	2.13*
5.	Introversion-extraversion	12.65	3.11	11.94	3.51	2.24*
6.	Masculinity- femininity	10.75	4.62	10.26	4.42	1.07
7.	Achievement Motivation	27.57	6.06	27.07	6.10	0.83
8.	Family Education Level	5.87	3.12	5.53	3.07	1.09
9.	Family Cultural Level	23.92	5.53	23.83	4.90	0.17
10.	Family Environment	16.81	4.52	16.73	4.57	0.18
11.	Family Acceptance	23.06	5.03	23.08	5.08	0.04
12.	Home Learning Facility	11.16	3.51	10.63	3.43	1.52
		$N_1 = 119$		$N_2 = 636$		

* Significant at 0.05 level ** Significant at 0.01 level

The above table shows that out of the twelve variables used in this study Introversion – extraversion and Examination Anxiety variables are capable of discriminating Discrepant Achievers (Under Achievers) and Non Discrepant Achievers in Social Studies at 0.05 level of significance. It can be seen that Discrepant Achievers (UA) have secured higher means than Non Discrepant Achievers in all the variables which discriminate the two groups. The discriminating variables in the order of importance are:

Introversion - extraversion (CR = 2.24)

Examination Anxiety (CR =2.13)

In all the remaining variables (Personal Adjustment, Social Adjustment, General Anxiety, Masculinity – femininity, Achievement Motivation, Family Education Level , Family Cultural Level, Family Environment, Family Acceptance and Home Learning Facility) the mean difference between Discrepant Achievers (Under Achievers) and Non Discrepant Achievers in Social Studies is not significant.

8. Comparison of Discrepant Achievers (Over Achievers) and Non Discrepant Achievers in Social Studies with respect to each of the Psychological and Familial variables

The statistical indices and the results of the tests of significance for the twelve Psychological and Familial variables for Discrepant Achievers (Over Achievers) and Non Discrepant Achievers in Social Studies are presented in Table 28.

The above table shows that out of the twelve variables used in this study, six variables are capable of discriminating Discrepant Achievers (Over Achievers) and Non Discrepant Achievers in Social Studies.

The discriminating variables in the order of importance are :

Family Education Level (CR = 6.87)

Home Learning Facility (CR = 5.31)

Masculinity – femininity (CR = 4.42)

Social Adjustment (CR = 2.64)

Achievement Motivation (CR = 2.44)

Personal Adjustment (CR = 1.99)

TABLE 28 : STATISTICAL DATA AND RESULTS OF TESTS OF SIGNIFICANCE FOR DIFFERENCE BETWEEN MEANS OF THE PSYCHOLOGICAL AND FAMILIAL VARIABLES DISCREPANT ACHIEVERS (OVERACHIEVERS) AND NON DISCREPANT ACHIEVERS IN SOCIAL STUDIES.

Variables		DA (OA)		NDA		Critical Ratio
		Mean M_1	S.D σ_1	Mean M_2	S.D σ_2	
1.	Personal Adjustment	54.39	10.42	52.36	10.36	1.99*
2.	Social Adjustment	52.76	12.08	49.69	10.65	2.64**
3.	General Anxiety	14.37	4.23	14.80	4.78	1.01
4.	Examination Anxiety	12.67	4.69	12.47	5.05	0.43
5.	Introversion-extraversion	12.38	3.67	11.94	3.51	1.23
6.	Masculinity- femininity	8.60	3.70	10.26	4.42	4.42**
7.	Achievement Motivation	28.58	6.33	27.07	6.10	2.44*
8.	Family Education Level	7.69	3.23	5.53	3.07	6.87**
9.	Family Cultural Level	24.69	4.67	23.83	4.90	1.86
10.	Family Environment	16.52	3.90	16.23	4.57	0.53
11.	Family Acceptance	23.02	4.17	23.08	5.08	0.14
12.	Home Learning Facility	12.27	3.09	10.63	3.43	5.31**
		$N_1 = 124$		$N_2 = 636$		

* Significant at 0.05 level **Significant at 0.01 level

Discrepant Achievers (Over Achievers) secured higher mean score than Non Discrepant Achievers in all the variables discriminating Discrepant Achievers (Over Achievers) and Non Discrepant Achievers in Social Studies except in Masculinity - femininity.

For the remaining variables, namely, General Anxiety , Examination Anxiety, Introversion – extraversion, Family Cultural Level, Family Environment and Family Acceptance the mean difference between Discrepant Achievers (Over Achievers) and Non Discrepant Achievers in Social Studies is not significant.

9. Comparison of Discrepant Achievers (Under Achievers) and Non Discrepant Achievers in Science with respect to each of the Psychological and Familial variables

Means of the Psychological and Familial variables of Discrepant Achievers (Under Achievers) and Non Discrepant Achievers were compared using two - tailed tests of significance. Information regarding the results of tests of significance for the different Psychological and Familial variables of Discrepant Achievers (Under Achievers) and Non Discrepant Achievers in Science are given in Table 29.

The above table shows that out of the twelve variables used in this study, three variables are capable of discriminating Discrepant Achievers (Over Achievers) and Non Discrepant Achievers in Science. Family Cultural Level and Home Learning Facility variables discriminate the two groups at 0.01 level of significance. Introversion – extraversion variable discriminates the two groups at 0.05 level of significance.

The discriminating variable in the order of importance are :

Home Learning Facility	(CR = 3.75)
Family Cultural Level	(CR = 3.17)
Introversion – extraversion	(CR = 1.99)

For all the three discriminating variables, Discrepant Achievers (Under Achievers) secured higher means than Non Discrepant Achievers.

TABLE 29 : STATISTICAL DATA AND RESULTS OF TESTS OF SIGNIFICANCE FOR DIFFERENCE BETWEEN MEANS OF THE PSYCHOLOGICAL AND FAMILIAL VARIABLES OF DISCREPANT ACHIEVERS (UNDER ACHIEVERS) AND NON DISCREPANT ACHIEVERS IN SCIENCE

	Variables	DA (UA)		NDA		Critical
		Mean	S.D	Mean	S.D	Ratio
		M_1	σ_1	M_2	σ_2	
1.	Personal Adjustment	52.97	12.14	51.96	9.89	1.75
2.	Social Adjustment	51.25	10.99	49.33	10.56	0.85
3.	General Anxiety	14.76	5.42	14.76	4.74	0.00
4.	Examination Anxiety	12.98	5.47	12.60	5.02	0.70
5.	Introversion-extraversion	12.55	3.29	11.89	3.39	1.99*
6.	Masculinity- femininity	9.81	4.05	10.34	4.47	1.28
7.	Achievement Motivation	27.55	6.05	27.06	6.07	0.81
8.	Family Education Level	6.13	3.04	5.56	3.13	1.86
9.	Family Cultural Level	25.08	4.97	23.50	5.00	3.17**
10.	Family Environment	17.41	4.33	16.58	4.58	1.89
11.	Family Acceptance	23.74	4.77	22.86	5.08	1.82
12.	Home Learning Facility	11.83	3.24	10.60	3.46	3.75**
		$N_1 = 118$		$N_2 = 635$		

* Significant at 0.05 level ** Significant at 0.01 level

In all the remaining variables (Personal Adjustment, Social Adjustment, General Anxiety, Examination Anxiety, Masculinity – femininity, Achievement Motivation, Family Education Level, Family Environment and Family Acceptance) the difference between means of Discrepant Achievers (Under Achievers) and Non Discrepant Achievers in Science is not significant.

10. Comparison of Discrepant Achievers (Over Achievers) and Non Discrepant Achievers in Science with respect to each of the Psychological and Familial Variables

The statistical indices and the results of the tests of significance for the twelve Psychological and Familial variable for Discrepant Achievers (Over Achievers) and Non Discrepant Achievers in Science are presented in Table 30.

TABLE 30 : STATISTICAL DATA AND RESULTS OF TESTS OF SIGNIFICANCE FOR DIFFERENCE BETWEEN MEANS OF THE PSYCHOLOGICAL AND FAMILIAL VARIABLES OF DISCREPANT ACHIEVERS (OVER ACHIEVERS) AND NON DISCREPANT ACHIEVERS IN SCIENCE

	Variables	DA (OA)		NDA		Critical Ratio
		Mean M_1	S.D σ_1	Mean M_2	S.D σ_2	
1.	Personal Adjustment	54.67	10.03	51.96	9.89	2.78**
2.	Social Adjustment	52.76	12.86	49.33	10.56	2.81**
3.	General Anxiety	14.64	4.21	14.76	4.74	0.29
4.	Examination Anxiety	12.57	4.65	12.60	5.02	0.07
5.	Introversion-extraversion	12.73	4.01	11.89	3.39	2.20*
6.	Masculinity- femininity	9.11	4.20	10.34	4.47	2.97**
7.	Achievement Motivation	28.60	6.48	27.06	6.07	2.46*
8.	Family Education Level	7.25	3.22	5.56	3.13	5.41**
9.	Family Cultural Level	25.22	4.39	23.50	5.00	3.92**
10.	Family Environment	16.72	3.99	16.58	4.58	0.35
11.	Family Acceptance	23.46	4.40	22.86	5.08	1.36
12.	Home Learning Facility	11.79	3.20	10.60	3.46	3.76**
		$N_1 = 126$		$N_2 = 635$		

* Significant at 0.05 level ** Significant at 0.01 level

From Table 30 it can be seen that out of the twelve variables used in this study six variables , namely, Social Adjustment, Personal Adjustment, Masculinity – femininity, Family Education Level , Family Cultural Level and Home Learning Facility are capable of discriminating Discrepant Achievers (Over Achievers) and Non Discrepant Achievers in Science at 0.01 level of significance. Introversion – extraversion and Achievement Motivation variables discriminate the two groups at 0.05 level of significance. It can be seen that Discrepant Achievers (OA) have secured higher means than Non Discrepant Achievers in all the discriminating variables except for the variable Masculinity -femininity.

The discriminating variables in the order of importance are :

Family Education Level	(CR = 5.41)
Family Cultural Level	(CR = 3.92)
Home Learning Facility	(CR = 3.76)
Masculinity – femininity	(CR = 2.97)
Social Adjustment	(CR = 2.81)
Personal Adjustment	(CR = 2.78)
Achievement Motivation	(CR = 2.46)
Introversion - extraversion	(CR = 2.20)

In all the remaining variables (General Anxiety, Examination Anxiety, Family Environment and Family Acceptance) the mean difference between Discrepant Achievers (Over Achievers) and Non Discrepant Achievers in Science is not significant.

11. Comparison of Discrepant Achievers (Under Achievers) and Non – Discrepant Achievers in Mathematics with respect to each of the Psychological and Familial variables

Means of the Psychological and Familial variables of Discrepant Achievers (Under Achievers) and Non Discrepant Achievers were compared using two - tailed tests of significance.

Information regarding the results of tests of significance for the different Psychological and Familial variables of Discrepant Achievers (Under Achievers) and Non Discrepant Achievers in Mathematics are given in Table 31.

TABLE 31 : STATISTICAL DATA AND RESULTS OF TESTS OF SIGNIFICANCE FOR DIFFERENCE BETWEEN MEANS OF THE PSYCHOLOGICAL AND FAMILIAL VARIABLES OF DISCREPANT ACHIEVERS (UNDER ACHIEVERS) AND NON DISCREPANT ACHIEVERS IN MATHEMATICS

	Variables	DA (OA)		NDA		Critical Ratio
		Mean M_1	S.D σ_1	Mean M_2	S.D σ_2	
1.	Personal Adjustment	52.76	9.82	52.01	10.26	0.78
2.	Social Adjustment	51.42	10.45	49.34	10.83	2.03*
3.	General Anxiety	14.41	4.81	14.92	4.77	1.09
4.	Examination Anxiety	11.98	5.09	12.88	4.98	1.82
5.	Introversion-extraversion	12.42	3.23	11.94	3.49	1.50
6.	Masculinity- femininity	10.03	3.95	10.32	4.51	0.74
7.	Achievement Motivation	27.81	5.76	26.99	6.14	1.44
8.	Family Education Level	6.62	3.42	5.44	2.98	3.61**
9.	Family Cultural Level	24.58	4.56	23.71	5.05	1.92
10.	Family Environment	16.62	4.25	16.73	4.56	0.26
11.	Family Acceptance	23.51	4.59	22.90	5.08	1.34
12.	Home Learning Facility	12.02	3.11	10.55	3.46	4.76**
		$N_1 = 125$		$N_2 = 661$		

* Significant at 0.05 level ** Significant at 0.01 level

The above table shows that out of the twelve variables used in this study, three variables are capable of discriminating Discrepant Achievers (Under Achievers) and Non Discrepant Achievers in Mathematics. Family Education Index and Home Learning Facility variables discriminate the two groups at 0.01 level of significance. Social Adjustment variable discriminates the two groups at 0.05 level of significance.

The discriminating variable in the order of importance are :

Home Learning Facility	(CR = 4.76)
Family Education Level	(CR = 3.61)
Social Adjustment	(CR = 2.03)

For all the three above discriminating variables Discrepant Achievers (Under Achievers) secured higher means than Non Discrepant Achievers.

In all the remaining variables (Personal Adjustment, General Anxiety, Examination Anxiety, Introversion – extraversion, Masculinity – femininity, Achievement Motivation, Family Cultural Level, Family Environment and Family Acceptance) the mean difference between Discrepant Achievers (Under Achievers) and Non Discrepant Achievers in Mathematics is not significant.

12. Comparison of Discrepant Achievers (Over Achievers) and Non Discrepant Achievers in Mathematics with respect to each of the Psychological and Familial variables

The statistical indices and the results of the tests of significance for the twelve psychological and familial variable for Discrepant Achievers (Over Achievers) and Non Discrepant Achievers in Mathematics are presented in Table 32.

From Table 32 it can be seen that out of the twelve variables used in this study six variables , namely, Social Adjustment, Personal Adjustment, Masculinity – femininity, Achievement Motivation , Family Education Level and Home Learning Facility are capable of discriminating Discrepant Achievers (Over Achievers) and Non

Discrepant Achievers in Mathematics at 0.01 level of significance. Introversion - extraversion and Family Cultural Level variables discriminate the two groups at 0.05 level of significance.

TABLE 32 : STATISTICAL DATA AND RESULTS OF TESTS OF SIGNIFICANCE FOR DIFFERENCE BETWEEN MEANS OF THE PSYCHOLOGICAL AND FAMILIAL VARIABLES OF DISCREPANT ACHIEVERS (OVER ACHIEVERS) AND NON DISCREPANT ACHIEVERS IN MATHEMATICS.

	Variables	DA (OA)		NDA		Critical Ratio
		Mean M_1	S.D σ_1	Mean M_2	S.D σ_2	
1.	Personal Adjustment	55.48	10.53	52.01	10.26	2.99**
2.	Social Adjustment	53.51	12.49	49.34	10.83	3.06**
3.	General Anxiety	13.94	4.52	14.92	4.77	1.94
4.	Examination Anxiety	11.89	5.21	12.88	4.98	1.72
5.	Introversion-extraversion	12.80	3.74	11.94	3.49	2.09*
6.	Masculinity- femininity	8.55	3.81	10.32	4.51	4.09**
7.	Achievement Motivation	29.26	6.35	26.99	6.14	3.24**
8.	Family Education Level	7.96	3.30	5.44	2.98	6.97**
9.	Family Cultural Level	24.88	4.70	23.71	5.05	2.23*
10.	Family Environment	16.72	4.11	16.73	4.56	0.02
11.	Family Acceptance	23.68	4.40	22.90	5.08	1.57
12.	Home Learning Facility	12.22	3.04	10.55	3.46	4.87**
		$N_1 = 93$		$N_2 = 661$		

* Significant at 0.05 level ** Significant at 0.01 level

The discriminating variables in the order of importance are :

Family Education Level (CR = 6.97)

Home Learning Facility (CR = 4.87)

Masculinity – femininity	(CR = 4.09)
Achievement Motivation	(CR = 3.24)
Social Adjustment	(CR = 3.06)
Personal Adjustment	(CR = 2.99)
Family Cultural Level	(CR = 2.23)
Introversion - extraversion	(CR = 2.09)

It is of interest to note that Discrepant Achievers (OA) have secured higher mean in all the above discriminating variables. In all the remaining variables (General Anxiety, Examination Anxiety, Family Environment and Family Acceptance) the difference between Discrepant Achievers (Over Achievers) and Non Discrepant Achievers in Mathematics is not significant.

A. Effectiveness of Psychological and Familial variables in Discriminating between Discrepant Achievers (Underachievers) and Non Discrepant Achievers in various school subjects.

An attempt has been made to study the effectiveness of the Psychological and Familial variables in discriminating Discrepant Achievers (Under Achievers) and Non Discrepant Achievers in various school subjects. A consolidated summary of the results is presented in Table 33.

It can be seen from Table 33 that Personal Adjustment discriminates between Discrepant Achievers (UA) and Non Discrepant Achievers only in one school subject Malayalam. Social Adjustment discriminates between DA (UA) and NDA in two school subjects, (viz;.) Malayalam and Mathematics. Examination Anxiety discriminates DA (UA) and NDA in two school subjects, Hindi and Social Studies. Introversion – extraversion discriminates DA (UA) and NDA in Social Studies and Science. Family Education Level discriminates DA (UA) and NDA in two school subjects, namely, English and Mathematics. Family Cultural Level discriminates DA (UA) and NDA only in one school subject, Science. Home Learning Facility discriminates DA (UA) and NDA in two school subjects,

Science and Mathematics. It is found that Non Discrepant Achievers in Malayalam scored higher means in Personal Adjustment and Social Adjustment than Discrepant Achievers (UA). Similarly, Non Discrepant Achievers in English scored higher means in Family Education Level than Discrepant Achievers (UA). For all other discriminating Psychological and Familial variables higher means are associated with Discrepant Achievers in all subjects than Non Discrepant Achievers.

TABLE 33: A CONSOLIDATED SUMMARY OF DISCRIMINATING PSYCHOLOGICAL AND FAMILIAL VARIABLES FOR DISCREPANT ACHIEVERS (UNDER ACHIEVERS) AND NON DISCREPANT ACHIEVERS IN DIFFERENT SCHOOL SUBJECTS

Variables	Malayalam	English	Hindi	Social Science	Science	Mathematics
Personal Adjustment	SS	NS	NS	NS	NS	NS
Social adjustment	SS	NS	NS	NS	NS	S
General Anxiety	NS	NS	NS	NS	NS	NS
Examination Anxiety	NS	NS	S	S	NS	NS
Intravenstion- extravenstion	NS	NS	NS	S	S	NS
Masculinity – femininity	NS	NS	NS	NS	NS	NS
Achievement Motivation	NS	NS	NS	NS	NS	NS
Family Education Level	NS	S	NS	NS	NS	SS
Family Cultural Level	NS	NS	NS	NS	SS	NS
Family Environment	NS	NS	NS	NS	NS	NS
Family Acceptance	NS	NS	NS	NS	NS	NS
Home Learning Facility	NS	NS	NS	NS	SS	SS

SS–Significant at 0.01 level; S–Significant at 0.05 level ; NS–Not significant

It is of interest to note that variables Masculinity –femininity, Achievement Motivation, Family Environment, General Anxiety and

Family Acceptance are not capable of discriminating between Discrepant Achievers (Under Achievers) and Non Discrepant Achievers in any school subject selected for study.

The discriminating variables have been arranged in the order of importance on the basis of the number of significant differences registered for the variable for six subjects. When the number of differences for any two variables are equal, the higher number of differences at the higher level (.01 level) was used as the basis for ranking the variable. The variables are presented in the order of importance in the list given below:

Home Learning Facility	(discriminates two groups; all at 0.01 level)
Family Education Level	(discriminates two groups; one at 0.01 level and one at 0.05 level)
Social Adjustment	(discriminates two groups; one at .01 level and other at 0.05 level)
Examination Anxiety	(discriminates two groups; all at 0.05 level)
Introversion-extraversion	(discriminates two groups; all at 0.05 level)
Family Cultural Level	(discriminates one group at the 0.01 level)
Personal Adjustment	(discriminates one group at the 0.01 level)

Discrepant Achievers (Under Achievers) and Non Discrepant Achievers in six school subjects and their corresponding discriminating Psychological and familial variables

The Psychological and Familial variables capable of discriminating between Discrepant Achievers (Under Achievers) and Non Discrepant Achievers in six school subjects are summarized below :

Group / Subject	Discriminating Variables
DA (UA) and NDA Malayalam	Personal Adjustment Social Adjustment
DA (UA) and NDA English	Family Education Level
DA (UA) and NDA Hindi	Examination Anxiety
DA (UA) and NDA Social Studies	Examination Anxiety Introversion - extraversion
DA (UA) and NDA Science	Introversion - extraversion Family Cultural Level Home Learning Facility
DA (UA) and NDA Mathematics	Social Adjustment Family Educational Level Home Learning Facility

It can be seen that as DA(UA) and NDA differ subject wise, the ability of the Psychological and Familial variables in discriminating the groups also differ. DA(UA) and NDA in Malayalam group is discriminated by two adjustment variables, viz; Personal Adjustment and Social Adjustment. DA (UA) and NDA in English is discriminated by Family Education Level and Hindi by Examination Anxiety. DA (UA) and NDA in Social Studies group is discriminated by Examination Anxiety and Introversion-extraversion. DA (UA) and NDA in Science is discriminated by three variables namely Introversion-extraversion, Family Cultural Level and Home Learning Facility. Similarly DA (UA) and NDA in Mathematics group is found to be discriminated by three variables, namely, Social Adjustment, Family Education Level and Home Learning Facility.

B. Effectiveness of the Psychological and Familial variables in Discriminating between Discrepant Achievers (Over Achievers) and Non Discrepant Achievers in various school subjects.

An attempt has been made to study the effectiveness of the Psychological and Familial variables in discriminating Discrepant Achievers (Over Achievers) and Non Discrepant Achievers in six school subjects. A Consolidated summary of the results is presented in Table 34.

TABLE 34 A CONSOLIDATED SUMMARY OF DISCRIMINATING PSYCHOLOGICAL AND FAMILIAL VARIABLES FOR DISCREPANT ACHIEVERS (OVER ACHIEVERS) AND NON DISCREPANT ACHIEVERS IN DIFFERENT SCHOOL SUBJECTS

Variables	Malayalam	English	Hindi	Social Science	Science	Mathematics
Personal Adjustment	NS	SS	NS	S	SS	SS
Social adjustment	SS	SS	SS	SS	SS	SS
General Anxiety	S	NS	NS	NS	NS	NS
Examination Anxiety	NS	NS	NS	NS	NS	NS
Introversion – extraversion	NS	SS	SS	NS	S	S
Masculinity – femininity	NS	SS	S	SS	SS	SS
Achievement Motivation	S	SS	NS	S	S	SS
Family Education Level	SS	SS	SS	SS	SS	SS
Family Cultural Level	NS	NS	NS	NS	SS	S
Family Environment	NS	NS	NS	NS	NS	NS
Family Acceptance	NS	NS	NS	NS	NS	NS
Home Learning Facility	SS	S	NS	SS	SS	SS

SS–Significant at 0.01 level; S – Significant at 0.05 level ; NS – Not significant

From the Table 34, it can be seen that Personal Adjustment discriminates between Discrepant Achievers (Over Achievers) and Non Discrepant Achievers in four school subjects (namely, English, Social Studies, Science and Mathematics).Social Adjustment discriminates between DA (OA) and NDA in all the six school subjects. General Anxiety discriminates between DA (OA) and NDA only in one subject ,Malayalam. Introversion – extraversion discriminates between DA (OA) and NDA in four school subjects , viz., English, Hindi, Science and Mathematics. Masculinity – femininity discriminates DA (OA) and NDA in five school subjects (English, Hindi, Social Studies, Science and Mathematics). Achievement Motivation discriminates between DA (OA) and NDA in five school subjects viz., Malayalam, English, Social Studies, Science and Mathematics). Family Education Level discriminates between DA (OA) and NDA in all the six school subjects. Family Cultural Level discriminates between DA (OA) and NDA in two school subjects (Science and Mathematics). Home Learning Facility discriminates between DA (OA) and NDA in five school subjects viz., Malayalam, English, Social Studies, Science and Mathematics.

It can also be seen from the above table that Examination Anxiety, Family Environment and Family Acceptance are not capable of discriminating between Discrepant Achievers (OA) and Non-Discrepant Achievers in any of the school subjects selected for study.

The discriminating variables between Discrepant Achievers (Over Achievers) and Non Discrepant Achievers have been arranged in an order of importance as mentioned earlier :

Family Education Level	(discriminates all the six groups; all at 0 .01 level)
Social Adjustment	(discriminates all the six groups; all at 0.01 level)
Home Learning Facility	(discriminates five groups; four at 0.01 level and one at 0.05 level)

Masculinity - femininity	(discriminates five groups; four at 0.01 level and one at 0.05 level)
Achievement Motivation	(discriminates five groups; (two at 0.01 level and three at 0.05 level)
Personal Adjustment	(discriminates four groups; two at 0.01 level and three at .05 level)
Introversion – extraversion	(discriminates four groups; two at 0.01 level and two at 0.05 level)
Family Cultural Level	(discriminates two groups; one at 0.01 level and one at 0.05 level)
General Anxiety	(discriminates one group at the 0.05 level)

Discrepant Achievers (Over Achievers) and Non Discrepant Achievers in six school subjects and their corresponding discriminating Psychological and Familial variables.

The Psychological and Familial variables capable of discriminating between Discrepant Achievers (Over Achievers) and Non Discrepant Achievers in six school subjects are summarized below :

It is seen that DA (OA) and NDA group in Malayalam are differentiated by five Psychological and Familial variables. DA (OA) and NDA in English group is differentiated by seven variables. DA (OA) and NDA in Hindi is differentiated only by four variables. DA (OA) and NDA in Social Studies is differentiated by six variables. The number and nature of variables that are capable of differentiating between DA (OA) and NDA are same for both Science and Mathematics groups.

Group / Subject	Discriminating Variables
DA (OA) and NDA Malayalam	Social Adjustment General Anxiety Achievement Motivation Family Educational Level Home Leaming Facility
DA (OA) and NDA English	Personal Adjustment Social Adjustment Introversion -extraversion Masculinity - femininity Achievement Motivation Family Educational Level Home Leaming Facility
DA (OA) and NDA Hindi	Social Adjustment Introversion -extraversion Masculinity - femininity Family Educational Level
DA (OA) and NDA Social Studies	Personal Adjustment Social Adjustment Masculinity - femininity Achievement Motivation Family Educational Level Home Leaming Facility
DA (OA) and NDA Science	Personal Adjustment Social Adjustment Introversion -extraversion Masculinity - femininity Achievement Motivation Family Educational Level Family Cultural Level Home Leaming Facility
DA (OA) and NDA Mathematics	Personal Adjustment Social Adjustment Introversion -extraversion Masculinity - femininity Achievement Motivation Family Educational Level Family Cultural Level Home Leaming Facility

CHAPTER 6

SUMMARY OF THE STUDY, CONCLUSIONS AND SUGGESTIONS

THE STUDY IN RETROSPECT

The present study was intended to compare Discrepant Achievers (Under Achievers and Over Achievers) and Non Discrepant Achievers in various school subjects (namely, Malayalam, English, Hindi, Social Studies, Science and Mathematics) with respect to certain Psychological and Familial variables. The study has been designed with 'discrepant – non discrepant continuum' as the dependent variable and twelve independent variables (seven Psychological and five Familial variables) as detailed below:

INDEPENDENT VARIABLES

Psychological Variables

Personal Adjustment

Social Adjustment

GENERAL ANXIETY

Examination Anxiety

Introversion-extraversion

Masculinity-femininity

Achievement Motivation

Familial Variables

Family Education Level

Family Cultural Level

Family Environment

Family Acceptance

Home Learning Facility.

HYPOTHESES

The study tested the following hypotheses:

I. Each of the independent variables selected for the study will discriminate significantly between Discrepant Achievers (Under Achievers) and Non Discrepant Achievers in six school subjects (namely, Malayalam, English, Hindi, Social Studies, Science and Mathematics).

II. Each of the independent variables selected for the study will discriminate significantly between Discrepant Achievers (Over Achievers) and Non Discrepant Achievers in six school subjects (namely, Malayalam, English, Hindi, Social Studies, Science and Mathematics).

OBJECTIVES

Based on the above hypotheses, the following objectives were formulated for the study.

(i) To compare each of the Psychological and Familial variables of Discrepant Achievers (Under Achievers) and Non Discrepant Achievers in six school subjects. The comparisons to be made for the following pairs separately :

DA (UA) - NDA (Malayalam)

DA (UA) - NDA (English)

DA (UA) - NDA (Hindi)

DA (UA) - NDA (Social Studies)

DA (UA) - NDA (Science)

DA (UA) - NDA (Mathematics)

(ii) To compare each of the Psychological and Familial variables of Discrepant Achievers (Over Achievers) and Non Discrepant Achievers (NDA) in six school subjects. The comparisons to be made for the following contrasted pairs :

DA (OA) – NDA (Malayalam)

DA (OA) – NDA (English)

DA (OA) – NDA (Hindi)

DA (OA) – NDA (Social Studies)

DA (OA) – NDA (Science)

DA (OA) – NDA (Mathematics)

PROCEDURE

The details of the procedure adopted are summarized below:

(a) Sample

The study used a representative sample of 879 secondary school pupils. The sample was confined to students attending standard IX drawn from representative schools of Kerala. The original sample was obtained using stratified sampling procedure with equal representation given to factors like school efficiency, rural – urban residence of subjects and sex of subjects. This basal sample was classified into Discrepant Achievers (Under Achievers and Over Achievers) and Non Discrepant Achievers in six school subjects using 'regression equations'.

(b) Tools

The study used the following standardized tools for measuring the Psychological and Familial variables.

- Kerala University Group Test of Intelligence (Verbal)
- The Kerala Non-verbal Group Test of Intelligence for secondary schools.
- Kerala Socio-personal Adjustment scale.
- Kerala Examination Anxiety Scale.
- Kerala General Anxiety Scale.
- The Kerala Introversion-extraversion scale.
- The Kerala Masculinity –femininity Scale.
- Kerala Scale of Achievement Motivation.
- Family cultural Level Rating Scale.
- Family Acceptance of Education Rating Scale.
- Home Learning Facility Inventory.
- General Achievement Tests for standard IX.
- Kerala Socio Economic Scale.

(c) Statistical techniques

(1) Discrepant Achievers in respect of each of the six school subjects were identified using Farquhar's regression technique.

(2) The data were analysed using two – tailed tests of significance of difference between means for large independent samples.

MAJOR FINDINGS OF THE STUDY

The study was designed to identify a group of Psychological and Familial variables which discriminate between Discrepant Achievers (Under Achievers and Over Achievers) and Non

Discrepant Achievers in six school subjects (namely, Malayalam, English, Hindi, Social Studies, Science and Mathematics).

The ability of the different Psychological and Familial variables to discriminate between Discrepant Achievers (Under Achievers and Over Achievers) and Non Discrepant Achievers was explored using Critical Ratio test. The major findings that emerged from the study have been summarized and presented below:

(i) Comparison of Discrepant Achievers (Under Achievers) and Non Discrepant Achievers (Malayalam)

Two Psychological variables, viz., 'Social Adjustment' and 'Personal Adjustment' discriminated significantly between DA (UA) and NDA in Malayalam. Non Discrepant Achievers secured higher means for both the discriminating variables.

(ii) Comparison of Discrepant Achievers (Over Achievers) and Non Discrepant Achievers (Malayalam)

Among the twelve Psychological and Familial variables, five variables, viz., 'Family Education Level', ' Social Adjustment', 'Home Learning Facility', ' General Anxiety' and 'Achievement Motivation' discriminated significantly between DA (OA) and NDA in Malayalam.

(iii) Comparison of Discrepant Achievers (Under Achievers) and Non Discrepant Achievers (English)

Among the twelve Psychological and Familial variables used in the study only 'Family Education Level' was capable of discriminating between DA (UA) and NDA in English.

(iv) Comparison of Discrepant Achievers (Over Achievers) and Non Discrepant Achievers (English)

Seven Psychological and Familial variables, viz., 'School Adjustment', 'Masculinity-femininity', 'Achievement Motivation', 'Family Education Level', 'Personal Adjustment', 'Introversion – extraversion', and 'Home Learning Facility' discriminated significantly between the contrasted groups DA (OA) and NDA in English.

(v) Comparison of Discrepant Achievers (Under Achievers) and Non Discrepant Achievers (Hindi)

Among the twelve Psychological and Familial variables, only 'Examination Anxiety' discriminated significantly between DA (UA) and NDA in Hindi.

(vi) Comparison of Discrepant Achievers (Over Achievers) and Non Discrepant Achievers (Hindi)

Four variables, viz., 'Family Education Level', 'Social Adjustment', 'Introversion-extraversion', and Masculinity – femininity' discriminated significantly between DA(OA) and NDA in Hindi.

(vii) Comparison of Discrepant Achievers (Under Achievers) and Non Discrepant Achievers in Social Studies

Among the twelve Psychological and Familial variables two variables, viz., 'Introversion – extraversion' and 'Examination Anxiety' discriminated between DA (UA) and NDA in Social Studies.

(viii) Comparison of Discrepant Achievers (Over Achievers) and Non Discrepant Achievers) in Social Studies

Six Psychological and Familial variables, viz., 'Family Education Level', 'Home Learning Facility', 'Social Adjustment', 'Achievement Motivation' and 'Personal Adjustment' discriminated between DA (OA) and NDA in Social Studies.

(ix) Comparison of Discrepant Achievers (Under Achievers) and Non Discrepant Achievers in Science

Among the twelve Psychological and Familial variables, only there variables, viz., 'Home Learning Facility', 'Family Cultural Level' and 'Introversion-extraversion' discriminated the contrasted pairs DA (UA) and NDA in Science.

(x) Comparison of Discrepant Achievers (Over Achievers) and Non Discrepant Achievers in Science

Eight Psychological and Familial variables , viz., 'Family Education Level', 'Family Cultural Level', 'Home Learning Facility',

'Masculinity -femininity', 'Social Adjustment', 'Personal Adjustment', 'Achievement Motivation' and 'Introversion – extraversion' discriminated between DA (OA) and NDA in Science.

(xi) Comparison of Discrepant Achievers (Under Achievers) and Non Discrepant Achievers in Mathematics

Out of the twelve Psychological and Familial variables, three variables, viz., 'Home Learning Facility', 'Family Education Level' and 'Social Adjustment' discriminated between DA (UA) and NDA in Mathematics.

(xii) Comparison of Discrepant Achievers (Over Achievers) and Non Discrepant Achievers in Mathematics

Out of the twelve Psychological and Familial variables eight variables, viz., 'Family Education Level', 'Home Learning Facility', 'Masculinity -femininity', 'Achievement Motivation', 'Social Adjustment', 'Personal Adjustment', 'Family Cultural Level' and 'Introversion - extraversion' discriminated between DA (OA) and NDA in Mathematics.

TENABILITY OF THE HYPOTHESES

Hypothesis I

"Each of the Independent variables selected for study will discriminate significantly between Discrepant Achievers (Under Achievers) and Non Discrepant Achievers in six school subjects (Malayalam, English, Hindi, Social Studies, Science and Mathematics)"

Among twelve Psychological and Familial variables three variables (Social Adjustment, Family Education Level and Home Learning Facility) discriminated DA(UA) and NDA (Mathematics), three variables (Introversion-extraversion, Family Cultural Level and Home Learning Facility discriminated DA (UA) and NDA (Science).

Out of twelve Psychological and Familial variables two variables (Personal Adjustment and Social Adjustment) discriminated DA (UA) and NDA groups Anxiety and Introversion-extraversion) discriminated DA (UA) and NDA (Social Studies). (Malayalam), two variables (Examination) Out of twelve independent variables only one variable (Family Education Level) discriminated DA (UA) and NDA (English); one variable (Examination Anxiety) alone discriminated between DA (UA) and NDA (Hindi).

Two-variables (Masculinity-femininity and Achievement Motivation) did not discriminate DA (UA) and NDA in any of the school subjects. Hence, we may conclude that the above hypothesis is only partially substantiated.

Hypothesis II

"Each of the independent variables selected for study will discriminate significantly between Discrepant Achievers (Over Achievers) and Non Discrepant Achievers in six school subjects (Malayalam, English, Hindi, Social Studies, Science and Mathematics)"

Out of the twelve Psychological and Familial variables eight variables (Personal Adjustment, Social Adjustment, Introversion-extraversion, Masculinity-femininity, Achievement Motivation, Family Education Level, Family Cultural Level and Home Learning Facility) discriminated DA (OA) and NDA (Mathematics); eight variables (Personal Adjustment, Social Adjustment, Introversion-extraversion, Masculinity-femininity, Achievement Motivation, Family Education Level, Family Cultural Level and Home Learning Facility) discriminated DA (OA) and NDA (Science).

Among the twelve Psychological and Familial variables, seven variables (Personal Adjustment, Social Adjustment, and Introversion –extraversion, Masculinity – femininity, Achievement Motivation, Family Education Level and Home Learning Facility) discriminated Discrepant Achievers (OA) and Non Discrepant Achievers in English. Six variables, namely, Personal Adjustment, Social Adjustment, Masculinity – femininity, Achievement Motivation, Family Education Level and Home Learning Facility discriminated Discrepant Achievers (OA) and Non Discrepant Achievers in Social Studies. Similarly of the twelve variables used in this study only five variables (Social Adjustment, General Anxiety, Achievement Motivation, Family Education Level and Home Learning Facility) discriminated between Discrepant Achievers (OA) and Non Discrepant Achievers in Malayalam. Again, four variables, viz; Social Adjustment, Introversion – extraversion, Masculinity –

femininity and Family Education Level discriminated between Discrepant Achievers (OA) and Non Discrepant Achievers in Hindi. Hence, we may conclude that the above hypothesis is mostly substantiated.

Suggestions for Improving Educational Practice

The present study is aimed at identifying a broad group of Psychological - Familial variables capable of discriminating between (i) Discrepant Achievers (Under Achievers) and Non Discrepant Achievers, and (ii) Discrepant Achievers (Over Achievers) and Non Discrepant Achievers in six school subjects. Besides the contribution of the study to theory, the conclusions also have some relevance to the improvement of educational practices. The Psychological and Familial variables which are identified as causal variables of underachievement in various school subjects are amenable for considerable educational modification so that the incidence of underachievement can be brought down to a considerable extent. Similarly, those variables, which are associated with overachievement, can also be modified for further enhancing the educational performance of over achievers. The following are certain suggestions for improving educational practice:

Two adjustment variables – Personal Adjustment and Social Adjustment – have been identified as causal factors of Discrepant Achievers (Over Achievers) and Non Discrepant Achievers in all the six school subjects. Both these variables can be classified under one broad head: socio - personal adjustment variables. Though there are various agencies, namely, the home and its environment, society in which the student is a member, other than the school, which determine a student's adjustment level, the school is supposed to be the most dominant determinant of a student's adjustment level. The pulls and pressures from numerous agencies may lead in developing many mental imbalances in the child. The school can reduce these imbalances by adopting suitable curricular and co-curricular activities such as:

(a) maintaining democratic classroom climate.

(b) adopting individualized instructional practices.

(c) avoiding certain situations in the school which may lead to intensification of maladjustment in children.

(d) adopting suitable measures to do away with children's hostility to school.

(e) identification of the causes of mal adjustment and treatment with the help of specialists.

(f) providing excellent guidance and counseling by experts

(g) constant interaction with parents so that they can provide timely advice

(h) education of the community to provide congenial learning atmosphere to the child

(i) providing opportunities to the child to develop their talents

(j) development of better teacher-student relationship in and out of the classroom

The fact that the higher the level of adjustment, the higher will be the level of achievement and vice versa should be interpreted in terms of cause – effect relationships. It is expected that a child who is capable of better personal and social adjustment is also capable of adjusting to different types of social pressure, social expectations, etc. A well-adjusted child develops intrinsic interest in the subject of his study and this enables him to achieve better. Further, he develops proper learning habits and this enables him to perform better at school. All these help the child to overcome difficulties and work for proper goals which he himself has set.

The study brought to light that Examination Anxiety is related to Discrepant Achievement (Underachievement). The defects in the present system of examination lead to the children developing examination anxiety. The whole system of education has become examination-oriented. It is argued that examination dictates the direction of education. The fear of detention, punishment etc. increases examination anxiety and this is turn leads to underachievement,. Instead of an external examination conducted at the end of the year, an alternate system of education, which creates the least examination anxiety in children, should be developed. Examination should never be used as a tool to punish children. On the other hand it should be used as a means of improving the techniques of learning and methods of teaching.

The study has revealed the effect of Family Education Level on Discrepant Achievement, Family Education Level stands for Education, Occupations and Income of Parents. The role of parents in the development of children is very important. Parental profession and parental income exercise considerable influence on the education of children. Students belonging to these groups have high socio – cultural environment, enhanced motivation and acceptances of academic values. Similarly high – parental education provides proper socio – cultural background to children. Children of well-educated parents are found to be good scholastic performers. This is due to the fact that these children have proper heredity and wholesome environment, which develop along with higher parental education. These are factors, which affect achievement considerably, and so higher parental profession, education and income act as variables affecting the achievement. So it is necessary to educate the parents on the need for a psychological approach to the adjustment problems of children. Though parental occupation and parental income are factors, which fall outside the purview of the educational practitioners who have little control over them. However, the education can create such conditions within the school, which would lead to the better performance of the children.

Psychological variables viz., personal adjustment, social adjustment, General Anxiety, Examination Anxiety, Introversion – extraversion, Masculinity – Femininity, Achievement Motivation have been found to discriminate between.Discrepant Achievers and Non Discrepant Achievers. This differentiation can be interpreted in two ways. One possibility is to assume that certain clusters of personality variables act as causal factors of under achievement and over achievement. Yet another way of interpreting the difference is to assume that achievement and the related different personality variables are connected by many intervening social and cultural variables like child rearing practices, attitude towards problem solving, cognitive styles etc.

Some of the psychological variables like Achievement Motivation can be presumed to be directly associated with discrepant achievement. It is possible to interpret the relationship noticed in the case of this variable by assuming that, other things remaining the same, the better a person's Achievement Motivation, the better will be his performance in problem solving situation of all kinds.

The above mentioned arguments are valid in interpreting the noticed relationship between Psychological variables like Social Adjustment, Masculinity – femininity, Introversion-extraversion and Achievement motivation. All these variables have the potential to cause achievement. Introversion, for example, implies self-analysis and possible weighing of consequences of possible action. The masculine disposition implies the displaying of unusual abilities or achieving what in generally thought to be unachievable. The noticed relationship between 'Masculinity – femininity and discrepant Achievement could perhaps be explained is terms of the above arguments. All these interpretations are tentative. Any confirmation of these interpretations requires further empirical studies, conducted with the specific intention in explaining these overlaps.

Social variables are seen to have the ability to discriminate between Discrepant Achievers and Non Discrepant Achievers. There are considerable research evidence which indicate that socio – cultural and family variables very similar to those identified by the study are related to achievement. Composite social – familial variables would influence creative performance either in the form of special family environment which better SES can provide or special forms of attitudes and dispositions and training that higher SES can generate, which in turn can augment the level of achievement. The fact that different components of SES influence such aspects as initial mental potential, rate of cognitive development, cognitive styles of subject suggest the possibility that they can also influence their achievement.

The relationship between Achievement and Family Education Level can be explained when we assume that the more educated a father, the better will be the cultural environment to which the child is exposed. Ordinarily, a more educated father will have better vocabulary, better attitude towards learning, more original ideas about solving problems and dealing with cognitive situations. The educated father and mother have a dominant influence on the child, as compared with other members of the family especially in the

Indian social context. Also, the father often exerts a significant influence on the achievement motivation of the child through proper guidance, type and quality of education provided to him. The variable 'Father's Occupation can itself influence the 'Family Environment' and 'Family Cultural Level'. In other words, all these variables as components of certain more generalized cultural and social variables that determined all kinds of mental performance. It is well accepted that discrepant achievement is very often decided by family environment and cultural level – the extent to which cognitive abilities are reinforced by other members of the family. Good home – environment with a good cultural background provides a better climate for the blossoming of a student with good academic abilities.

In the present study adjustment variables – Personal Adjustment and Social Adjustment – Examination Anxiety, Family Education Level Introversion-extraversion, Home Learning Facility and Family Cultural Level are found to be associated with Under Achievers and Non Discrepant Achievers. Comparison of independent variables between Under Achievers and Non Discrepant Achievers in six-school subject revealed the absence of a common set of discriminating variables between UA and NDA in all six-school subjects. From this we may conclude that the school subjects that a student studied have some association to the Psychological and Familial variables used in the study.

Also, the observed relationship between Psychological and Familial variables with discrepant achievers belonging to different school subjects, need more elaborate investigation before we can arrive at more satisfactory explanations of the associations. Though the study helps us to indicate the association between the experimental variables and discrepant achievers in various school subjects, it is not comprehensive enough to provide adequate information that will help us to infer the exact or real cause of such associations subject – wise. The interpretations attempted above are what the investigator considers to be most plausible from the obtained information. A comprehensive factor study of the above variables with discrepant achievers and non-discrepant achievers for different school levels will possibly provide some more information regarding the overlaps.

An attempt was made to find out – though it was not an objective of the present study - consistent Discrepant Achievers, that is, consistent Under Achievers (Under Achievers in all the six school subjects selected in this study) and consistent Over Achievers (Over Achievers in all the six school subjects selected for the present study). Among the 879 samples used in the present study it was seen that 13 students (1.47%) were found underachieving consistently and 6 students (0.68%) were found to be overachieving consistently. So it may be may concluded that Under Achiever in one school subject need not be always an Under Achiever in another school subject. Similarly Over Achiever in one school subject need not be always an Over Achiever in another school subject. Hence it can be concluded that the school subjects have a great influence in deciding Discrepant Achivement.

Contributions of the study

The present investigation has helped to identify some major Psychological and Familial variables, which are capable enough to discriminate discrepant achievers and non-discrepant achievers in various school subjects. The findings of the present study have wide implication for theory making in respect of discrepant achievement, for developing better practices in relation to identification, prediction and development of overall achievement of pupils. The important implication are given below:

(a) Developing a more dependable theory relating to achievement of discrepant achievers and non discrepant achievers.

The present study has helped to identify a broad group of Psychological and Familial variables related to discrepant achievement and non discrepant achievement. The findings of the present study would help to develop a broader theory of performance of discrepant achievers and non discrepant achievers in different school subjects, which will include cognitive, affective and familial variables.

Variables which prominently figure in the list of discriminating variables pose new questions about the distribution of these variables among students belonging to underachievement, overachievement categories. A stable theory of discrepant achievement thus formulated may help us in (i) defining the concept of discrepant achievement, (ii) understanding its psychometric structure (iii) suggesting possible remedy methods and developing intervention of educational strategies for fostering it.

It is further possible to conduct a more focused series of investigations on these lines and develop more comprehensive theories about the nature and characteristics of discrepant and non discrepant achievement among students.

(b) Identification and prediction of discrepant behaviour

The identified Psychological and Familial variables are helpful to educators in understanding the difference, which exist between discrepant achievers and non discrepant achievers. Psychometric prediction equation can be worked out by treating the prominent discriminating variables identified by the study. It is possible to develop different equations for different groups of Under Achievers, Over Achievers and Normal Achievers and establish convenient out – off points for classifying, students into different groups. One of the prediction equations will help to identify discrepant achievement early enough and provide suitable remedial or enrichment programmes.

(c) Developing new instructional strategies for dealing with discrepant achievers

The identified Psychological and Familial variables discriminating between discrepant achievers and Non Discrepant achievers will help to understand the differing levels of students on academic achievement. This suggests the possibility of devising new instructional or other types of intervention strategies for fostering talent among underachievers. Once the overachieving group of students is identified, it is possible to think of focused strategies that will help to increase the variables that have strong positive association with overachievement. Educationists, interested in fostering achievement, can workout strategies that will increase the effect of the discriminating variables which are liable to improvement like 'Achievement Motivation' 'Adjustments' etc: such practices are likely to augment achievement of underachievers. It needs to be stressed that the Psychological variables associated with the two groups – underachievers and overachievers – are capable of modified through a sound system of education or through appropriate forms of educational treatment. It is also possible to manipulate the immediate cultural environment of a pupil so as to achieve the effects produced by educated fathers and mothers, increase the learning facility at home, etc. Hence strategies that will help to increase a set of Psychological and Familial variables will possibly be a new or improved instructional strategy in dealing with discrepant achieves in various school subjects. Special guidance programme, group work, etc. can be looked upon as additional strategies for fostering achievement. We can also think of giving the equivalent of parental education through special counseling for parents and making them more efficient in dealing with their wards. Again, we can develop a cadre of special teachers for various school levels with special competence and expertise in dealing with discrepant achievers. They can be used as resource persons for different schools. Their services can be used to help the ordinary teacher in identifying and dealing with discrepant achievers with special reference to underachievers. A strategy for increasing the level of achievement of discrepant achievers will have to be worked out and used by these researchers.

Suggestions for further research

On the basis of the present study the investigator would like to offer certain suggestions for further study. While such suggestions can not be regarded as very exhaustive and complete, an attempt has been made to test some areas of most immediate interest to this investigator hereunder :

1. Replication of the present study with other personality, psychological and social variables for various school subjects.

2. Replication of the present study to compare the two groups of discrepant achievers namely underachievers and overachievers with respect to various personality , psychological and social variables.

3. The present study was conducted on secondary school pupils . The study could be aimed at for students of other educational levels – primary, higher secondary and degree levels.

4. Factorial comparison of personality , psychological and social factor structures of over, normal – and underachievers with a view to obtaining a broader picture of the groups.

5. A follow – up study of the persistence of discrepant achievement in various subjects at different educational levels to answer such basic questions like the following: Does an underachiever at one level continue to be an underachiever through out his educational career? does an overachiever at one educational level become an underachiever at some advanced level?

It is hoped that the study has brought to light some useful information regarding the nature of variables that can discriminate discrepant achievers from Non Discrepant achievers in various school subjects.

Bibliography

BOOKS

Agarwal, S.K. (1975). A Psychosocial study of academic underachievement at Secondary School Level in the state of Rajasthan (Doctor al Thesis in Education, Rajasthan University) as citied in M.B.Buch (sd), *A Third Survey of Research in Education*, New Delhi, NCERT, 1986 P.657.

Albert, R.S (Ed.).(1992). *The Social Psychology of Creativity and Exceptional Achievement.* (2nd ed.). New York: Pergamon..

Beedawat, S.S. (1976). A Study of Academic Under-Achievement Among Students in *Second Survey of Research in Education*, M.B. Buch (ed.), Baroda: Society for Educational Research and Development, 1979, p. 343.

Bhatt, K.K. (1971). Adjustment problems of Over – and Underachiever, in *Second Survey of Research in Education*, M.B. Buch (ed.), Baroda: Society for Educational Research and Development, 1979, 00. 172 – 173.

Best, John W. and Khan, James V. (1996) *Research in Education (7th ed.)* Newdelhi: Prentice Hall of India Private Limited, P. 137-217.

Burns, Robert. B. (2000). *Introduction to Research Methods (4th ed.).* New Delhi: Sage Publications Inc.

Chaudhari, V.P., Jain. (1975). Factors contributing to Academic Under-achievement in *Third Survey of Research in Education*, M.B. Buch (ed.), New Delhi: National Council of Educational Research and Training, 1986. P.600.

Cruickshank, W.M. and Johnson, G.O. (1974). *Education of Exceptional Children and Youth.* Englewood Cliffs, N. J., prentice Hall, Inc.

Cryer, Pat. (1999). *The Research Students Guide to Success.* New Delhi: Viva Books Pvt. Ltd.

Dhaliwal, A. S. (1971). A Study of some factors contributing to Academic Success and failure among High School students – Personality Correlates of Academic Over, and Under – achievement, in *Second Survey of Research in Education*, M. B. Buch (ed.), Baroda: Society for Educational Research and Development, 1974, p. 329.

Dhami, G.S. (1974). Intelligence, Emotional Maturity and Socio-economic Status as Factors Indicative of Success in scnolastic Achievement, in *Third Survey of Research in Education.* M.B. Buch (ed.), New Delhi: National Council of Educational Research and Training, 1986, pp. 662 – 663.

Downie, N.M & R.W. Health (1970). *Basic Statistical Methods.* (3rd ed.) New York : Harper & Row.

Ebel, Robert and Frishic, David A (1991) *Essentials of Educational Measurement.* (5th ed.), New Delhi: Prentice Hall of India Pvt. Ltd.

Farwell, G.F. and Peters, H. J. (1961). *Guidance Reading for Counselors.* Chicagao : R and Mcnally and Company.

Garrett, H.E. (1966). *Statistics in Psychology and Education.* Bombay: Vakils, Feffer and Simon, P. Ltd.

Getzels, J.W. and Jackson, P.W. (1962). *Creativity and Intelligence.* New York: John Wiley and Sons.

Ghuman, M.S. (1976). A Study of Aptitudes, Personality Traits and Achievement Motivation of Academic Over-achievers and Under-achievers, in *Third Survey of Research in Education*, M.B. Buch (Ed.), Baroda: A Centre of Advanced Study in Education, 1986, pp. 664 – 665.

Girden, Ellen R. (1996). *Evaluating of Research Articles From Start to Finish.* New Delhi: Sage Publications.

Glatthorn, Allan A. (1998). *Writing the Winning Dissertation; A Step-by step Guide.* California: Crowin Press, Inc.

Gupta, P.L. (1983). A Study of Personality Characteristics of Ninth Grade Over – and Underachieving Boys and Girls at Different Levels of Achievement motivation, in *Fourth Survey of Research in Education*, M.B. Buch (ed.), New Delhi: National Council of Educational Research and Training, 1991, p.

Guilford, J.P. (1954). *Psychometric Method.* New York: Mc Graw – Hill paradigmatic behaviourism: screening and identification of high – potential under- Book Company, Inc.

Jagannadhan, K. (1985). The effect of certain socio – psychological factors on the academic achievement of children studying in class V to Class VII. in *Fourth Survey of Research in Education*, M. B. Buch (ed.), New Delhi: NCERT, 1991, p. 826.

Lavin, D.E, (1965). *The Prediction Academic Performance*, New York: Russel Sage Foundation, 1965.

Maitra, K. (1985). Affective Correlates of the Gifted Underachievers, in *Third Survey of Research in Education,* M.B. Buch (ed.), Baroda: A Centre of Advanced Study in Education, 1986, P.834.

Mehrotra.s. (1986). A study of the relationship between Intelligence, socio-economic status, anxiety, Personal Adjustment and Academic Achievement of High School Students. Doctoral Thesis, Kanpur University. *Fourth Survey of Research in Education.*New Delhi: NCERT, 1991.

Miller, L.M. (1968). *Guidance for the Underachiever with superior ability.* Washington, D.C. : U.S. Department of Health, Education, and Welfare.

Mike Card well (1991) *The complete A-Z Psychology Hand book.* London: Hodder & Stoughton.

Nagpal, R. (1979). A Study of Non-intellectual characteristics of over and underachieving Engineering students, in *Third Survey of Research in Education,* M.B. Buch (Ed.), Baroda : A Center of Advanced Study in Education, 1986, PP-678.

N M Downie & R.W. Helath (1970) Baric statistical Methods (3rd Ed.). New York : Herper. V. Row.

Otto, et al . (1973). Corrective and Remedial Teaching. Boston: Houghton Mifflin Company: 1973

Puri, K. (1987). Personality Traits and Self concept of 16-18 years old underachievers, in *Fourth Survey of Research in Education,* M.B. Buch (ed.), New Delhi : National Council for Educational Research and Training, 1991, P.845.

Salunke, R.B. (1979). A Study of the Home Environment, Socio-economic Status and Academic Management in relation to the Academic Achievement of the First Year College Students of M.S. University, in *Third Survey of Educational Research,* M.B. Buch (ed)., Baroda : A Center of Advanced Study in Education, 1986, P P. 685-686.

Sathyanandam, B.D. (1969). A Study of Socio-economic Status and Academic Achievement in *Third Survey of Research in Education,* M.B. Buch (ed)., New Delhi : National Council of Educational Research and Training, 1986.

Sharma, K.G. (1972). A Comparative Study of adjustment of Over and Underachievers, *Survey of Research in Education,* M.B. Buch (ed.),

Baroda : A Center of Advanced Study in Education, 1974, P P. 344-345.

Skinner, Charks E. (1995). *Educational Psychology:* New Delhi: Prentice Hall of Indian, Pvt Ltd.

Tandon, S. (1978). A Psychological and Ecological Study of Underachiever, in *Second Survey of Research in Education,* M.B. Buch (Ed.), Baroda : Society of Educational Research and Development, 1979, P. 361.

Taylor, C.W. (ed.), (1964). *Creativity : Progress and Potential.* New York : MC Graw-Hill Book Company.

Thorndike, R.L. (1963). *The concept of Over and Underachievement.* New York : Bureau of Publications, Teacher's College, Columbia University.

Thorndike, R.M. (1991) *Measurement and Evaluation in Psychology and Education (5th ed.).* New York: Macmillan Publishing Co.

Torrance, E.P. (1962). *Guiding Creative Talent.* New Delhi : Prentice- Hall of India.

Vanarase, S.J. (1970). Ability and Scholastic Underachievement, in *A Survey of Research in Education,* M.B. Buch (ed.), Baroda : A Center of Advanced Study in Education, 1978, P P. 348-349.

Vernon, P.E. (1972). *The Measurement of Abilities.* London : University of London press.

Wellington, C.B. and Wellington, J. (1961). *The Underachiever : Challenges and Outlines.* Chicago : Rand MC Nally and Company.

Wellington, C.B. and Wellington, J. (1964). *The Underachiever : Challenges and Guidelines.* Chicago : Rand MC Nally Curriculum Series, Rand MC Nally and Company.

JOURNALS

Abraham, Mercy. (1972). A Comparative Study of the Incidence of Under achievement and Overachievement in English in Government and Private Schools of Kerala, *Kerala Journal of Education,* (International Book Year Special), 4, 18 –22.

Abraham, Mercy. (1973). Effect of Intelligence and study Habits on English Achievement at Secondary Level, *Journal of Educational Research and Extension,* 9, 171-177.

Abraham, Mercy. (1975). Age and Sex as Factors of Under achievement in English at Secondary School Stage, *Studies in Education*, 8, 31– 38.

Barrett, H. G. (1957). Intensive Study of Thirty two Gifted Children, *Personnel and Guidance Journal*, 35, 192-194.

Barrett, H.G. (1965). Attributes of Pupils Achieving beyond their Level of Expectancy, *Journal of Educational Psychology*, 59, 10.

Biggers, Maureen Short.(1990). The impact of a multifaceted intrusive psychoeducational intervention on underachieving college freshmen, Abstract. *Dissertation Abstracts International*, 51 : 12.

Blusiewiez, C. O. (1983). The Association of Locus of Control and Future Time Orientation with Achievement and Under achievement, Abstract. *Dissertation Abstracts International*, 44: 1381.

Burt, C. (1966). The Genetic Determination of Difference in Intelligence: A Study of Monozygotic Twins Reared Together and Apart, *British Journal of Educational Psychology*, 57, 137 – 153.

Colemaw,W and E.E.Cureton (1954).Intelligence and Achievement: The Gangle ifallacy'again. *Educational and Psychological Measurement* 14: 347-357.

Cruickshank, W.M. and Johnson, G.O.(1974). *Education of Exceptional Children and Youth*. Englewood Cliffs, N. J., prentice Hall, Inc.

Davis, J.A and F.Norman, "Public and Private School Graduates in Colleges", *Journal of Teacher Education* 16:18-12, 1955.

Deo, P. and Gupta, A.K. (1972). A Comparison of the Criteria for Identifying over – and underachievers, *Indian Educational Review*, 7, 236.

Desana, P. A. (1966). Problems of consistent over, Under and Normal achieving College Students as Identified by the Money Problem Check – list, *Journal of Educational Research*, 59, 351 – 355.

Dhaliwal, A.S. and Saini, B.S. (1976). Relationship of Creativity with Academic Over, Under – achievement, *Psychological Studies*, 21, 30 – 39.

Donald V. Forrest. (1967). High School Underachievers in College, *The Journal of Educational Research*, 61 (4), 147 – 149.

Dutt, Sunil. (1988). Relationship of Creativity with achievement in Science and Socio – economic Status of X Grade students, *Journal of Educational Research and Extension*. 25 (2) : 106 – 111.

Fink, M.B. (1962). Self-concept as it Relates to Academic Underachievement, *California Journal of Educational Research*, 13, 57 – 62.

Flores, John Robert. (1989). The effects of Cross-age tutoring on under – achieving fifth grade students in the areas of mathematical achievement and self – perception, Abstract. *Dissertation Abstracts International*, 50 : 11.

Ford, Donna Yvette. (1991). Self – perceptions of Social, Psychological and Cultural Determinants of achievement among gifted Black students : A Paradox of under-achievement, Abstract. *Dissertation Abstracts International*, 52 : 7.

Frankel, E. (1960).A Comparative Study of the Achieving and Underachieving High School Boys of High Intellectual Ability, *Journal of Educational Research*, 53, 172 – 180.

Gilmore, J.V. (1968). The Factor of Attention in Underachievement, *Journal of Education*, 150, 41 – 66.

Goldberg, M. L. (1955). A Three Year Experimental Progress at Dwitt Clinton High School to Help Bright Underachievers, *High Points*. 41, 5 – 35.

Gold berg, M.L. (1959). A Three-Year Experimental Progress at Dwitt Clinton High School to Help Bright Under Achievers, *High Points*, 41,5-35.

Gough, H.C. (1955). Dynamics of Underachievement of Gifted Students, *Exceptional Children*, 24, 98 – 101.

Gowan, J.C. (1957). Dynamics of the Underachievement of Gifted Students, *Exceptional Children*, 24, 98 – 101.

Gowan, J.C. (1964). Underachievement Revisited, *High School Journal*, 48, 117 – 119.

Grant, Kenneth, Dalton (1986). The Characteristics of the Home Environment of High Achieving and Low Achieving Twelfth Grade. *Dissertation Abstracts International*. 47 (2):1276.

Hammel, R. amd Sprinthall, N. (1965). Underachievement related to Interests, Attitudes and Values, *The Personnel and Guidance Journal*, 44, 388 – 395.

Hishinuma, E.S.(1990). A theoretical and pragmatic application of paradigmatic behaviourism: screening and identification of high – potential under-achievers currently in regular education, Abstract. *Dissertation Abstracts International*, 51: 5.

Irvine, Donald, W. (1966). Relationships between the STEP Tests and Overachievement / Underachievement, *The Journal of Educational Research,* 59.

Jaganadhan, K (1986). A Study on the Home Environment and Academic Achievement. *Journal of Educational Research and Extension,* 23:18-24.

Janice M. Barwick and Dugald S. Arbuckle. (1962). A Study of the Relationship between parental Acceptance and the Academic Achievement of Adolescents, *The Journal of Educational Research,* 56 (3), 148 – 151.

Jeon, Kyung-Won. (1989). Perceptions of American Teachers, American Parents, Korean teachers and Korean parents of the gifted under-achueving gifted, Abstract. *Dissertation Abstracts International,* 50 : 11.

John,J.Bibb.(1974). Achievement Motivation Test Anxiety and Under achievement in the Elementary School, *The Journal of Educational Research,* 67, 366-368.

Joshi, J.N. and Sharma, R. (1968). Role of Non-intellectual Factors in Underachievement, *NIE Journal,* NCERT, 4,9

Kaile, Harnek S. and Tejinder Kaur Punia. (!993). Relationship Between Creativity and Socio-economic Status, *Experiments in Education.* 21 (12) : 304-308.

Kamala S. Pillai. (1987). Certain Family Environmental Variables causing Underachievement in Mothertongue of Secondary School Students, *Journal of Educational Reasearch and Extension,* 23 (3), 129-132.

Kaul, B.N. (1968). Raising Academic Standards of Underachievers : Report on an Action Research, *NIE Jounal (NCERT),* 2, 58-60.

Kelso, Jane (1991). Home Environment Correlates of Achievement, Aptitude and Behaviour in elementary School Child, Ph.D, The University Lowa, *Dissertation Abstracts International,* 52(10): 3562 A.

Kemmerer, Ann Herd. (1987). A Study of ego, intellectual and identity development in underachieving and high-achieving college freshmen, Abstraact. *Dissertation Abstracts International,* 48 : 7.

Klein, Jerome. (1984). Underachievement : The Two Type Hypothesis, Abstract. *Dissertaion Abstracts international,* 45; 464.

Lohani, Ira and Mohite, Prema (1990) Link between selected Family Demographic selected family Demographic factors, Home Environment and Academic performance. *Perspectives in Education* 6: 119-124.

Lum, K.M. (1960). A Comparison of Underachieving and Overachieving Female College students, *Journal of Educational psychology*, 51 (2), 109-114.

Marrow, W.R. and Wilson, R.R. (1961). Family Relations of Bright High-achieving and Underachieving High School Boys, *Child Development*, 32, 501-510.

Matlin A.H. and P.A. Mendelsohn. (1965). The Relationship between Personality and Achievement Variables in the Elementary Schools, *Journal of Educational Research*, 58: 457-459.

Michael E. Osborn. (1971). The Impact of Differing Parental Educational level on the Educational Achievement, Attitude, Aspiration and Expectation of the Child, *The Journal of Educational Research*, 65 (4), 163-166.

Mitchell, J.V.(1959) "Goal-setting Behaviour as a Function of Self-acceptance, Over-and Under-achievement and Related Personality Variables", *Journal of Educational Psychology*, 50:93-106, 1959.

Mohan, V. and Nehru, K. (1972). Differentiation of Over and Underachievers on 16 PF, *Psychological Studies*, 17, 52-55.

Nair, A.S. (1981). Some Social-familial Variables causing underachievement in Secondary School Mathematics, *Journal of Education and Extension*, 18, 10-13.

Najma, S. and Satyanarayan, B.S. (1978). Test anxiety among High School Children, *Quest in Education*, 15, 120-126.

Natesan, Hemalatha and Seetha, R..(1986). Achievement Motivation and Academic Achievement, *Journal of Educational Research and Extension*, 23, 48.

Peters, Cheryl Oberg. (1991). Attitude Profiles of Gifted achieving, gifted underachieving and nongifted middle school students, Abstract. *Dissertation Abstracts International*, 52 : 5.

Rai, P.N (1979). A comparative study of adjustment and scholartic achievement of low and high achievers. *Quest in Education* 15:111-112

Rao, G.D. (1970). Study of Some Factors Related to Scholastic Achievement, *Indian Journal of Psychology*, 45, 99-120.

Reeder, A.L. and Conger, R.D. (1984). Differential Mother and Father Influences on the Educational Attainment of Black and White Women, Abstract. *Sociological Abstracts*, 32 : 1170.

Roberts, H.E.(1962). Factors Affecting the Academic Underachievement of Bright High School Students, *Journal of Educational Research*, 56, 175-183.

Sena, Paul A. De. (1966). Problems of Consistent Over, Under and Normal Achieving Colleges Students as Identified by the Money problem Check List, *The Journal of Educational Research*, 59 (8), 351-355.

Sharma, S. (1978). A Study of Relationship of General and Test Anxiety to Scholastic Attainment in Different Courses as a Function of Intelligence, *Quest in Education*, 15, 128-132.

Shaw, G.B. (1966). Causes of Underachievement in Mathematics- An Inquiry, *Education and Psychology Review*, 6, 79-87.

Singh, B. and P.Kumar (1977) Anxiety and Educational Achievement. *Journal of Psychological Research*. 21, 56-59.

Srivastava, V. (1990). A Study of the Effect of Family Environment on Students Achievement. *Journal of Psychological Researchers*, 35(2):87-91.

Srivasturah. (1969). Ability and Under-achievement, *Indian Educational Review*, 4, 116-122.

Stix, Daniel T. (1976). Discrepant Achievement in College as a function of Anxiety and Repression, *The Personal and Guidance Journal*, 48 (8).

Taylor, R.G. (1964). Personality Traits and Discrepant Achievement : A Review, *Journal of Counseling Psychology*, 11, 76-82.

Tolor, Alexander. (1969). Incidence of Underachievement at the High School Level, *The Journal of Educational Research*, 63, 63-65.

Torrance, E.P. (1962). "Who is the Underachiever ?", *National Educational Association Journal*, 51, 14-17.

Uchat, D.A. (1987). A Comparative Study of Underachievers and Overachievers on the basis of Certain Personal and Family Related Factors, *Journal of Educational Research and Extension*, 23, 160-168.

DISSERTATIONS

Abraham, Mercy (1969). *An Investigation into the Relationship Between certain Environmental variables and underachievement in English of secondary school pupils of Trivandrum city.* Masters Dissertation; University of Kerala

Anandavally, T. (1972). *A Study on the Inter – relationship Between Intelligence, Achievement, Socio – of the Higher Secondary School Pupils in Kerala.* Master's Dissertation, University of Kerala.

Bhaduri, A. (1971). *A Comparative Study of Certain Psychological Characteristics of the over – and Underachievers in Higher Secondary Schools.* Doctoral dissertation, Calcutta University.

Cherian, S. (1984). *A Study of the problems faced by Underachievers in Secondary Schools.* Unpublished Master's Dissertation. University of Kerala.

Indu, K.S. (1996). *A Study on the Influence of Family Climate and Family Assistance on the Achievement in English of Secondary School Pupils.* Master's Dissertation, University of Kerala.

Iyer, R.K. (1977). *Some Factors Related to Underachievement in Mathematics of Secondary School Students.* Unpublished Doctoral dissertation, University of Kerala.

Jayagopal, R. (1974). *Personality profile of the Under and High – Achievers of some of the schools in the city of Madras. Madras*: Department of Psychology, Madras University.

John, P. and Abraham, M. (1981). *A Study of underachievement among college students with a view to formulating a guidance profile,* Master's Dissertation, Department of Education, Kerala University.

Joseph, Magdaline. (1977). *Inter-personal Attitudes Associated with underachievement of High School Pupils.* Master's Dissertation University of Kerala.

Kurup, Gopalakrishna, P.S. (1969). *Factorial Validity of the Kerala University Verbal Group Test of Intelligence.* Master's Dissertation, University of Kerala.

Lalithamma, K.N. (1975). *Some Factors Affecting Achievement of Secondary Pupils in Mathematics.* Doctoral Dissertation, University of Kerala.

Mathew, T. (1975). *Some Personality Factors Related to Underachievement in Science.* Un-published Doctoral dissertation University of Kerala.

Menon, S.K. (1973). *A Comparative Study of the Personality Characteristics of Over-achievers and Under achievers of High Ability.* Doctoral Dissertation, Department of Psychology, Kerala University.

Nair, N. Jagannadhan. (1974). *Identification of Some Variables which Discriminate between High Intelligence Normal Achievers and High Intelligence Underachievers in Mathematics.* Master's Dissertation, University of Kerala.

Nair, P.M. (1975). *Personal Characteristics of Creative High School Pupils.* Doctoral Dissertation, Kerala University.

Nair, P.V. (1979). *A Comparative Study of the Cognitive and Affective Factor Structures of High and Low Science Achievers in Secondary Schools.* Master's Dissertation, University of Kerala.

Nair, Viswanadhan, P. (1987). *A Comparative Study of certain cognitive and social variables which discriminate between high-creative and low-creative underachievers in secondary school science.* Doctoral Dissertation, University of Calicut, Kerala.

Parvathy, V. (1984). *Certain Sociological Factors Discriminating Underachievers and Non-Underachievers in Secondary School Malayalam.* Master's Dissertation, University of Calicut.

Pearlman, Samuel. (1960). *An Investigation of the problems of Academic Underachievement among Intellectually superior college students.* Ph.D. Thesis, New York University.

Rekha, M.K. (1994). *A study of the Relationship between Home Environment and Achievement in Science of Lower Primary Pupils.* Unpublished MEd Thesis, University of Kerala.

Sathi, P. (1973). *Personality Factors of Underachievers and Overachievers of High Ability.* Doctoral Dissertation, University of Kerala.

Saxena, P.C. (1972). *A Study of Interests, Need Patterns and Adjustment problems of Over and Underachievers.* Doctoral Dissertation, University of Allahabad.

Soman, K. (1977). *Some Affective Correlates of Mathematics Achievement of Secondary School Students.* Doctoral Dissertation, University of Kerala.

Somasundaram, M.A. (1980). *Comparative Study of Certain Personality Variables related to Over, Normal and Under-achievement in Secondary School Mathematics.* Doctoral Dissertation, Calicut University, Kerala.

Usha, N.S. (1986). *Extent of Successive Academic Gap in Learning Science in High Schools and its Relationship between Learning Environment.* Master's Dissertation, University of Kerala.

Haq, Najmul. (1988). *A Study of certain Personality Correlates of Over achievements and Under achievement in different School Subjects.* Doctoral Dissertation, Aligarh Muslim University, Aligarh.

Nair,Sankaran. (1984). *Factors Related to Underachievement in biology of Secondary School Students.* Doctoral Dissertation, University of Calicut, Calicut.

TOOLS

Nair, A.S. (1968). *The Kerala Non-verbal Group Test of Intelligence for Secondary Schools.* Trivandrum: Department of Education, University of Kerala.

Nair, A.S. (1976). *Kerala Examination Anxiety Scale.* Department of Education, University of Kerala.

Nair, A.S. (1976). *Kerala Scale of Achievement Motivation.* Trivandrum : Department of Education, University of Kerala.

Nair, A.S. (1976). *Kerala Socio-Personal Adjustment Scale.* Trivandrum : Department of Education, University of Kerala

Nair, A.S. (1976). *The Kerala Introversion-extraversion Scale.* Trivandrum : Department of Education, University of Kerala.

Nair, A.S. (1979). *The Kerala Masculinity-Femininity Scale.* Trivandrum : Department of Education, University of Kerala.

Nair, A.S. (1980). *The Kerala Socio-economic Scale.* Trivandrum : Department of Education, University of Kerala.

Nair, A.S. and Devi, Nirmala. (1981). *Home Learning Facility Inventory.* Calicut : Department of Education, University of Calicut.

Nair, A.S. and Devi, Nirmala. (1981). *Family Acceptance of Education Rating Scale.* Calicut : Department of Education, University of Calicut.

Nair, A.S. and Devi, Nirmala. (1981). *Family Environment Index Inventory.* Calicut : Department of Education, University of Calicut.

Nair, A.S. and Devi, Nirmala. (1981). *Family Cultural Level Rating Scale.* Calicut : Department of Education, University of Calicut.

Pillai, N.P., Nair, A.S. and Amma, J.G. (1968). *Kerala University Test Intelligence* (Verbal). Trivandrum : Department of Education, University of Kerala.

OTHERS

Chen etal (1995). "Motivation and Mathematics Achievement. A comparative Study of Asian-American, Caucasian-American and East Asian High School students ". *ERIC* Record 56(46) Child-Development; V66n4 p1215-34 Aug.1995.

Husen, Torston and Postleth Waite, Neville T. (1996). *The International Encyclopedia of Education.* (2nd . ed.), Great Britain: BPC Wheaton Ltd.

Jayagopal, R. (1974). *Personality profile of the Under and High – Achievers of some of the schools in the city of Madras. Madras*: Department of Psychology, Madras University.

Klinger,-Barbara; Nelson,-Denise (1996) "Improving Academic Achievement of At-Risk students in English Education and Key boarding I", 56(11),119.*ERIC* Document Reproduction Service.

Miller, L.M. (1968). Guidance for the Underachiever with superior ability. Washington, D.C. : U.S. Department of Health, Education, and Welfare.

Nord, Christine - Winquist (1998). "Students Do Better when Their Fathers Are Involved at School Issue Brief" 56(2), 3. *ERIC* Document Reproduction Service.

Paul, Grayson.J. (1996). "Under- and Over-Achievement in First year " 56(6), 31.*ERIC* Document Reproduction Service. ED 404904.

Reeder, A.L. and Conger, R.D. (1984). Differential Mother and Father Influences on the Educational Attainment of Black and White Women, Abstract. *Sociological Abstracts,* 32: 1170.

Report of the Education Commission (1964-66). New Delhi : Ministry of Education, Government of India.